I0567309

Every possible effort has been made to ensure that the information contained in this book is accurate at the time of going to press, and the publishers and the author cannot accept responsibility for any errors or omissions, however caused. No responsibility for loss or damage occasioned to any person acting, or refraining from action, as a result of the material in this publication can be accepted by the publisher or the author.

www.toptenaward.org

595

Canadian Citizenship
Practice Tests

First Edition

Plus Online Test:
www.toptenaward.org

Mahnaz Waezi

Vancouver, BC CANADA

Published by: Top Ten Award International Network Inc.

Vancouver, BC **CANADA**
Email: Info@TopTenAward.Net
www.toptenaward.net

Ordering Information:
Quantity sales. Special discounts are available on quantity purchases by universities, schools, corporations, associations, and others. For details, contact the "Sales Department" at the above mentioned email address.

595 Canadian Citizenship Tests, Mahnaz Waezi, 1st ed.
ISBN: 978-1-990451-71-3   Paperback

This book is dedicated to my late mum, Setareh

1- Which one of the following is not a source of Canadian law?

A) Laws passed by Parliament

B) Civil code of France

C) English common law

D) Military code of France

2- What does the Great Charter of Freedom include?

A) Freedom of conscience and religion

B) Employment rights

C) Aboriginal Peoples' rights

D) Freedom from taxes

3- Which one of the following is not included in the Great Charter of Freedom?

A) Freedom of thought, belief, opinion, and expression.

B) Freedom of conscience and religion

C) Freedom to buy property

D) Freedom of association

4- Who can enter and leave the country freely without time constraints?

A) Canadian citizens

B) Canadian citizens and landed immigrants

C) British citizens

D) Commonwealth citizens

5- Which three rights are included in the Canadian Charter of Rights and Freedoms?

A) Mobility rights, Aboriginal Peoples' rights, and official language rights

B) Freedom of expression rights, property rights and fair trial rights

C) Employment rights, mobility rights, and freedom rights

D) Aboriginal Peoples' rights, voting rights and official language rights

6- Which one of the following is a responsibility of Canadian citizenship?

A) Buying a piece of land

B) Helping others in the community

C) Serving in the Army

D) Camping

7- When called to do so, serving on a jury is:

A) A legal requirement

B) An option

8- In Canada, what does "equality of men and women" mean?

A) Men and women can both perform housework

B) Men and women are equal under the law

C) Men and women must both drive a vehicle

D) Women must earn more money

9- Which part of the Constitution summarizes fundamental freedoms while also setting out additional rights?

A) The Canadian Charter of Rights and Freedoms

B) The Canadian Charter of Rights

C) The Canadian Charter of Freedoms

D) The British Charter of Rights and Freedoms

10- As a Canadian citizen, in which elections do you have a responsibility to vote?

A) Federal, provincial or territorial and local elections

B) Federal, provincial or territorial elections

C) Local elections only

D) Federal elections only

11- Canada is not the only constitutional monarchy in North America

A) True

B) False

12- What is the key phrase in Canada' s original constitutional document?

A) Peace, Order and Good Government

B) Work, Order and Good Government

C) Peace, Order and Mobility Rights

D) Government, Work and Good Order

13- What is the name of Canada' s original constitutional document?

A) The British North America Act

B) The Constitutional Act

C) The Legislative Act

D) The Confederation Act

14- Name three beliefs that have enabled Canadians to build a prosperous society in a rugged environment.

- A) Ordered liberty, enterprise and buying houses

- B) Enterprise, hard work and driving cars

- C) Hard work, fair play and ordered liberty

- D) Outdoor life, hard work, and fair play

15- What kind of commitment do Canadian institutions uphold?

- A) Peace, Order, and Good Government

- B) Work, Order and Good Government

- C) Peace, Order, and Mobility Rights

- D) Work, Order, and Good Government

16- As what have poets and songwriters hailed Canada?

- A) The "Great Dominion"

- B) The "Land of the Brave"

- C) The "Great Outdoors"

- D) "Peace, Order and Good Government"

17-Who are the three founding peoples of Canada?

A) Aboriginal, Métis and Inuit

B) British, Métis and Aboriginal

C) Aboriginal, French, and British

D) Early settlers, Métis and Inuit

18- From where were the ancestors of Aboriginal peoples believed to have migrated?

A) Europe

B) Africa

C) Australia

D) Asia

19- Aboriginal and Treaty rights are not in the Constitution

A) True

B) False

20- When were Aboriginal territorial rights first guaranteed?

A) 1759

B) 1659

C) 1749

D) 1763

21- Who proclaimed the first territorial right guarantee for the First Nations?

A) King George III

B) King George II

C) King George I

D) Queen Elizabeth

22- When did the federal government place many Aboriginal children in residential schools?

A) From the beginning of the 1900s until the 1980s

B) From the 1700s until the 1980s

C) From the 1800s until the 1980s

D) From the 1700s until the 1970s

23- To what does the term "Indians" refer?

A) Métis and Inuit

B) Acadians, Métis and First Nations

C) All aboriginal peoples who are not Inuit or Métis

D) Early settlers, Métis and Inuit

24- When did the term "First Nations" begin to be used?

A) In the 1970s

B) In the 1960s

C) In the 1980s

D) Never

25- How many First Nations people live on reserve land today?

A) About two thirds

B) About half

C) About one third

D) 100%

26- What are the three main groups of Aboriginal peoples?

A) First Nations, Métis and Inuit

B) Acadians, Métis and First Nations

C) French, English and First Nations

D) Early settlers, Métis and Inuit

27- Who was John Buchan?

A) A popular Governor General of Canada

B) A famous Canadian general

C) A victorious Canadian army General

D) One of the Fathers of Confederation

28- What was the view on immigration of John Buchan, a popular Governor General of Canada in the 1930s?

A) Complete cultural assimilation

B) No unity

C) No diversity

D) Unity in diversity

29- What does the word "Inuit" mean?

A) "The people"

B) "The land"

C) "The village"

D) "The far North"

30- Where do Inuit people live?

A) In scattered communities across the Arctic

B) In small towns across Manitoba

C) Across the Yukon

D) In reserve land across the Northwest Territories

31- Who are the Métis?

A) A distinct people of mixed Aboriginal and European ancestry

B) First Nations

C) Acadians

D) Inuit

32- Where does the majority of the Métis live?

A) Atlantic provinces

B) Prairie provinces

C) Western provinces

D) Northern provinces

33-What is the speaking background of the Métis population?

A) French

B) English

C) Both French and English

D) Acadian

34- What is the name of Metis dialect?

A) Acadian

B) Michif

C) Frenglish

D) Inuit

35- Which group of Aboriginal peoples has the largest population in Canada?

A) Inuit

B) Métis

C) First Nations

D) Acadians

36- What are Canada's two official languages?

A) English and First Nations

B) English and French

C) French and British

D) First Nations and French

37- The federal government is required by law to provide services throughout Canada in

A) English and French

B) Chinese and English

C) English only

D) English, French and Chinese

38- Who are Anglophones?

A) People who speak English as a first language

B) People who speak French as a first language

C) Aboriginal people who speak English as a first language

D) British people

39- Who are Francophones?

A) Aboriginal people who speak French as a first language

B) People who speak English as a first language

C) French people

D) People who speak French as a first language

40- How many Anglophones are there in Canada today?

A) 18 million

B) 50 million

C) 10 million

D) 5 million

41- How many Francophones are there in Canada today?

A) 10 million

B) 5 million

C) 7 million

D) 50 million

42- In which province does the majority of Francophones live?

A) Alberta

B) New Brunswick

C) Manitoba

D) Quebec

43- Which province is the only official bilingual province?

A) Alberta

B) New Brunswick

C) Manitoba

D) Quebec

44- Acadians are the descendants of what groups?

A) Métis and Inuits

B) French colonists who began settling in what are now the Maritime provinces in 1604

C) First Nations who began settling in what are now the Prairie provinces in 1600s

D) British colonists who began settling in what are now the Maritime provinces in 1604

45- What was the "Great Upheaval"?

A) The deportation of more than two-third of Acadians from their homeland between 1755 and 1763

B) The deportation of more than two-third of Aboriginal from their homeland between 1755 and 1763

C) The deportation of more than two-third of Inuit from their homeland between 1755 and 1763

D) The great earthquake that ravaged Canada's East Coast during the 18th century

46- What are Quebecers?

A) The Acadians

B) The francophones

C) The French-speaking Aboriginals

D) The people of Quebec

47- Quebecers are the descendants of what groups?

A) British colonists who began settling in the 1600s in what are now the Maritime provinces

B) Métis and Inuit

C) French settlers from the 1600s and 1700s

D) Acadians

48- Who recognized in 2006 that the Quebecois form a nation within a united Canada?

A) The Prime Minister

B) The House of Commons

C) The Senate

D) The Cabinet Ministers

49- When did the House of Commons recognize that the Quebecois form a nation within a united Canada?

A) 2006

B) 2001

C) 1986

D) 1972

50- In becoming Canadian, which principles are newcomers expected to embrace?

A) Democratic

B) Libertarian

C) Liberalist

D) Capitalist

51- Who were the English-speaking settlers?

A) English, Welsh, Scottish and Métis

B) Australians and British

C) English, Irish and French

D) English, Welsh, Scottish and Irish

52- Who are generally referred to as "English Canadians"?

A) The English-speaking Aboriginals

B) The Anglophones

C) The British

D) The English

53- Since the 1800s, where were the majority of Canadians born?

A) China

B) India

C) Canada

D) England

54- Regarding diversity, as what is Canada often referred?

A) The land of the strong and free

B) The Great Dominion

C) A land of immigrants

D) The Great Outdoors

55- Since the 1970s, from where do most immigrants come from?

A) Asia

B) Europe

C) South America

D) Africa

56- After English, what is the second most-spoken non-official language in Canadian homes?

A) Punjabi

B) Chinese

C) French

D) Spanish

57- To which religious affiliation do the great majority of Canadians identify?

A) Christian

B) Muslim

C) Jewish

D) Hinduism

58- Who is Marjorie Turner-Bailey?

A) An Olympian and descendant of black Loyalists

B) A famous Canadian settler

C) The first woman to become Prime Minister

D) The first Canadian female athlete

59- In Canada, gays and lesbians enjoy the full protection of and equal treatment under the law, including access to civil marriage

A) True

B) False

60- Which of the following statements about residential schools is false?

A) Aboriginal people demanded to be placed in residential schools

B) The schools were poorly funded and inflicted hardship on the students

C) Aboriginal language and cultural practices were mostly prohibited

D) The federal government placed many Aboriginal children in residential schools to educate and assimilate them into mainstream Canadian culture

61- Which natives were hunter-gatherers?

A) The Cree and Dene of the Northwest

B) Huron-Wendat of the Great Lakes region and the Iroquois

C) The Sioux

D) The Inuit

62- When did English settlement begin in Canada?

A) 1510

B) 1497

C) 1610

D) 1720

63- When did European exploration begin in Canada?

A) 1497

B) 1510

C) 1610

D) 1597

64- When did English colonies appear along the Atlantic seaboard?

A) The early 1600s

B) The mid 1600s

C) The late 1600s

D) The early 1700s

65- Who led thousands of Loyalist Mohawk Indians into Canada in 1776?

A) Robert Baldwin

B) Joseph Brant

C) Joseph Howe

D) Sir John A. Macdonald

66- Which current provinces came out from the Constitutional Act?

A) Ontario and New Brunswick

B) Prince Edward Island and Quebec

C) Ontario and Quebec

D) Ontario and Prince Edward Island

67- When did the name "Canada" become official?

A) 1758

B) 1889

C) 1609

D) 1791

68- Who made Upper Canada the first province in the British Empire to abolish slavery?

A) Joseph Brant

B) Joseph Howe

C) Lieutenant Colonel John Graves Simcoe

D) Sir John A. Macdonald

69- When did the British Parliament abolish slavery throughout the Empire?

A) 1833

B) 1807

C) 1853

D) 1793

70- When did the United States launch an invasion on Canada?

A) 1812

B) 1840

C) 1867

D) 1849

71- Which countries fought in the War of 1812?

A) United Kingdom and United States of America

B) France and Canada

C) United States of America, France and United Kingdom

D) France and United Kingdom

72- In which year did the American attempt to conquer Canada fail?

A) 1814

B) 1840

C) 1867

D) 1849

73- In what year did Canada become a country?

A) 1840

B) 1982

C) 1759

D) 1867

74- In what year were Upper and Lower Canada united?

A) 1840

B) 1882

C) 1759

D) 1867

75- Who became the first leader of a responsible government in the Canadas?

A) La Fontaine

B) Robert Baldwin

C) Joseph Howe

D) Sir John A. Macdonald

76- What does "Confederation" mean?

A) The joining of several provinces to form a new country

B) The joining of several British colonies to form a new country

C) The joining of several cities to form a new province

D) The split between the South and the North

77- When did the British Parliament pass the British North America Act?

A) 1840

B) 1982

C) 1759

D) 1867

78- When is Canada Day?

A) First of July

B) First of November

C) 11th of November

D) 11th of September

79- Who assigned Canada's national colours (white and red) in 1921?

A) King George V

B) King George II

C) King James

D) Queen Victoria

80- Who suggested the term, "Dominion of Canada" in 1864?

A) La Fontaine

B) Robert Baldwin

C) Joseph Howe

D) Sir Leonard Tilley

81- Which phrase embodied the vision for the Dominion of Canada?

A) "Oh Canada, my home and native land"

B) "Dominion from sea to sea and from the river to the ends of the earth"

C) "Dominion from ocean to ocean"

D) "The land of the free and strong"

82- In which year was Canada's first Prime Minister elected?

A) 1964

B) 1764

C) 1867

D) 1869

83- Who was Canada's First Prime Minister?

A) Sir John Alexander Macdonald

B) Sir George-Étienne Cartier

C) Sir Louis-Hippolyte La Fontaine

D) Sir Étienne-Paschal Taché

84- Whose portrait is on the Canadian $10 bill?

A) Sir George-Étienne Cartier

B) Sir Louis-Hippolyte La Fontaine

C) Sir Étienne-Paschal Taché

D) Sir John Alexander Macdonald

85- Who was the key architect of Confederation from Quebec?

A) Sir George-Étienne Cartier

B) Sir Louis-Hippolyte La Fontaine

C) Sir Étienne-Paschal Taché

D) Sir John Alexander Macdonald

86- When did Canada take over the vast northwest region from the Hudson's Bay Company?

A) 1949

B) 1869

C) 1864

D) 1905

87- When was the RCMP created?

A) 1864

B) 1869

C) 1873

D) 1892

88- What does "RCMP" stand for?

A) Royal Canadian Mounted Police

B) Royal Canadian Master Police

C) Registered Canadian Mounted Police

D) Registered Canadian Municipal Police

89- What is the Royal Canadian Mounted Police?

A) A national police force

B) A municipal police force

C) army police

D) A provincial police force

90- The British territories in the Caribbean Sea are part of Canada.

A) True

B) False

91- Who became the first French-Canadian prime minister since Confederation?

A) Sir Wilfrid Laurier

B) Sir Étienne-Paschal Taché

C) Sir Louis-Hippolyte La Fontaine

D) Sir George-Étienne Cartier

92- Whose portrait is on the $5 bill?

A) Sir George-Étienne Cartier

B) Sir Wilfrid Laurier

C) Sir Étienne-Paschal Taché

D) Sir Louis-Hippolyte La Fontaine

93- What made it possible for immigrants to settle in Western Canada?

A) The completion of the port of Vancouver

B) The completion of the Canadian National Railway

C) The giving of free land to new settlers

D) The completion of the Canadian Pacific Railway

94- How many Canadians served in the First World War?

A) About 60,000

B) About 170,000

C) About 10,000

D) More than 600,000

95- Who had the reputation of being the "shock troops of the British Empire"?

A) The Canadian troops

B) The French troops

C) The British troops

D) The Caribbean troops

96- Who was Canada's greatest soldier during the First World War?

A) Lt. Col. John McCrae

B) General Sir Alexander Macdonald

C) General Sir Arthur Currie

D) Colonel Sir Joseph Howe

97- What is known as the women's suffrage movement?

A) The effort by women to end suffering

B) The effort by women to achieve the right to vote

C) The feminist movement

D) The war liberation movement by women

98- When were most Canadian female citizens, aged 21 and over, granted the right to vote in federal elections?

A) 1918

B) 1921

C) 1889

D) 1945

99- Who was the founder of the women's suffrage movement?

A) Agnes Macphail

B) Dr. Emily Stowe

C) Thérèse Casgrain

D) Marie Howe

100- When is Remembrance Day?

A) First of November

B) 11th of November

C) 11th of September

D) 21st of December

101- What is the meaning of the Remembrance Day poppy?

A) To remember our Sovereign Queen Elizabeth II

B) To celebrate Confederation

C) To honour prime ministers who have died

D) To remember the sacrifice of Canadians who have served or died in wars up to the present day

102- What do Canadians remember on Remembrance Day?

A) The sacrifices of veterans and brave fallen in all wars

B) Canada's victory in the First World War

C) Canada's victory in the Second World War

D) Canada's first settlers

103- What do Canadians wear on Remembrance Day?

A) Red poppy

B) Blue ribbon

C) Red ribbon

D) Red bracelet

104- What was the name of the free association of states that the British Empire had evolved into after the First World War?

A) The British Commonwealth of Nations

B) The British Empire

C) The British Armed Nations

D) The British Colonial Dominion

105- When was the Bank of Canada created?

A) 1934

B) 1939

C) 1942

D) 1945

106- What led to the Great Depression in the 1930s?

A) The stock market crash of 1932

B) Low grain prices and a terrible drought in 1929

C) The stock market crash of 1929

D) Low grain prices and a terrible drought in 1932

107- In the epic invasion of Normandy in northern France in 1944, known as D-Day, which beach did the Canadians capture?

A) Juno

B) Omaha

C) Utah

D) Gold

108- During the Second World War, what was the ratio of Canadians in the Allied forces on D-Day?

A) 1 in 10

B) 1 in 5

C) 1 in 3

D) 1 in 2

109- How many Canadians served in the Second World War?

A) About 600,00

B) About 300,000

C) About 900,000

D) More than one million

110- Who contributed more to the Allied air effort than any other Commonwealth country during the Second World War?

A) England

B) Canada

C) India

D) Australia

111- What began Canada's modern energy industry in 1947?

A) The discovery of hydro-electricity in British Columbia

B) The Energy Bill passed by the House of Common

C) The discovery of coal in Manitoba

D) The discovery of oil in Alberta

112- When were the majority of Canadians able to afford adequate food, shelter and clothing for the first time?

A) 1945

B) 1949

C) 1951

D) 1954

113- Why do Canadians enjoy one of the world's highest standards of living?

A) By working hard and by trading with other nations

B) By working hard and by being a NATO member

C) Thanks to the NAFTA agreement

D) Thanks to the Americans

114- When was introduced Unemployment insurance (now called "employment insurance")?

A) 1940

B) 1927

C) 1965

D) 1970

115- When was Old Age Security devised?

A) 1940

B) 1927

C) 1965

D) 1970

116- When were the Canada and Quebec Pension Plans devised?

A) 1940

B) 1927

C) 1965

D) 1970

117- Canada is not a member of the North Atlantic Treaty Organization (NATO)

A) True

B) False

118- Canada is a member of the United Nations (UN)

A) True

B) False

119- What was the "Quiet Revolution"?

A) An era of rapid change in the 1960s in Quebec

B) The Cold War between the East and the West

C) The coming of the Old Age Security in Canada

D) The development of Canada's autonomy in the world after the Second World War

120- Which Act guarantees French and English services in the federal government across Canada?

A) The French Language Act

B) The English Language Act

C) The Bilingual Act

D) The Official Languages Act

121- What are the two official languages of Canada?

A) French and English

B) Chinese and English

C) English and Inuit

D) English and British

122- What is "La Francophonie"?

A) A region in Quebec

B) A French music instrument

C) An international association of French-speaking countries

D) A French music festival

123- Quebec enjoys sovereignty in Canada

A) True   B) False

124- When did the Japanese-Canadians gain the right to vote?

A) 1960

B) 1949

C) 1948

D) 1953

125- When were Aboriginal people granted the right to vote.

A) 1960

B) 1949

C) 1961

D) 1948

126- By the 1960s, how many Canadians had origins that were neither British nor French?

A) Half

B) One-third

C) Two-third

D) One-quarter

127- Who were the Group of Seven?

A) Seven Canadian greatest war heroes

B) The Father of the Confederation

C) The Seven Canadian best hockey players

D) Seven Canadian visual art artists who developed a certain style of painting

128- Who were pioneers of modern abstract art in the 1950s?

A) "Les Automatistes" of Quebec

B) The Abstractists

C) "Les Reformateurs" of Quebec

D) The Group of Seven

129- Basketball was invented by a Canadian

A) True

B) False

130- Why is Terry Fox a Canadian national hero?

A) He inspired people to contribute money for cancer research

B) He became the first elected President of Canada

C) He was the greatest hockey player of all time

D) He united Canada in the 19th century

131- What is often referred to as "the goal heard around the world"?

A) the winning goal for Canada in the Canada-Soviet Summit Series in 1992

B) the winning goal for Canada in the Canada-USA Summit Series in 1972

C) the winning goal for Canada in the Canada-Soviet Summit Series in 1972

D) the winning goal for Canada in the Canada-Soviet Stanley Cup Series in 1972

132- Which Canadian circled the globe in a wheelchair to raise funds for spinal cord research?

A) Terry Fox

B) Rick Hansen

C) Wayne Gretzky

D) Marshall McLuhan

133-Canadian football is absolutely identical to American football

A) True

B) False

134- Who invented the telephone?

A) Alexander Graham Telus

B) Alexander Graham Rogers

C) Alexander Graham Shaw

D) Alexander Graham Bell

135- Who invented the snowmobile?

A) Joseph-Armand Bombardier

B) Joseph-Armand Skidoo

C) Mike Lazaridis

D) Matthew Evans

136- Who invented the worldwide system of standard time zones?

A) Sir Sandford Fleming

B) Sir John A. Hopps

C) Sir Sandford Greenwich

D) Sir Henry Woodward

137- Who is known as "the greatest living Canadian"?

A) Sir Sandford Fleming

B) Terry Fox

C) Dr. Wilder Penfield

D) Sir John A. Macdonald

138- Insulin was discovered by a Canadian

A) True

B) False

139- Who invented the first cardiac pacemaker?

A) Sir Sandford Fleming

B) Dr. John A. Hopps

C) Dr. Wilder Penfield

D) Sir John A. Macdonald

140- The Blackberry is a Canadian invention

A) True   B) False

141- When did Canada enjoy one of the strongest economies among industrialized nations?

A) Between 1945 and 1970

B) Between 1925 and 1960

C) Between 1980 and 1990

D) Between 1970 and 1980

142- When did Canada draw closer to the United States and other trading partners?

A) Between 1925 and 1960

B) Between 1980 and 1990

C) Between 1945 and 1970

D) Between 1970 and 1980

143- What does the Canada Health Act ensure?

  A) Common elements and a basic standard of coverage

  B) Drinkable water for all Canadians

  C) No more contagious epidemics in Canada

  D) Publicly funded education

144- What was the name of the war that began when several liberated countries of Eastern Europe became part of a Communist bloc controlled by the Soviet Union?

  A) The Soviet War

  B) The Cold War

  C) The Eastern War

  D) The Union War

145- When did the Parliament establish the Royal Commission on Bilingualism and Biculturalism?

  A) 1945

  B) 1969

  C) 1963

  D) 1970

146- Who invented Basketball?

A) James Naismith

B) Donovan Bailey

C) Wayne Gretzky

D) Terry Fox

147- Who created insulin?

A) Dr. John A. Hopps

B) Dr. Wilder Penfield

C) Sir Frederick Banting of Toronto and Charles Best

D) Sir Sandford Fleming and Charles Best

148- Which famous Canadian artist painted the forests and Aboriginal artifacts of the West Coast?

A) Jean-Paul Riopelle

B) Emily Carr

C) Louis-Philippe Hébert

D) Kenojuak Ashevak

149- Who pioneered modern Inuit art?

A) Louis-Philippe Hébert

B) Emily Carr

C) Kenojuak Ashevak

D) Jean-Paul Riopelle

150- Which of the following is a person of letters who had a significant cultural impact?

A) Sir Ernest MacMillan

B) Kenojuak Ashevak

C) Pauline Johnson

D) Jean-Paul Riopelle

151- Which of the following is a Canadian musician who won renown in Canada and abroad?

A) Emile Nelligan

B) Sir Ernest MacMillan

C) Joy Kogawa

D) Jean-Paul Riopelle

152- Which of the following is a writer who has diversified Canada's literary experience?

A) Michael Ondaatje

B) Healey Willan

C) Louis-Philippe Hébert

D) Denys Arcand

153- Who was a celebrated sculptor of historical figures?

A) Kenojuak Ashevak

B) Norman Jewison

C) Emily Carr

D) Louis-Philippe Hébert

154- Whose films have been popular in Quebec and across the country, and have won international awards?

A) The films of Louis Hémon

B) The films of Louis-Philippe Hébert

C) The films of Denys Arcand

D) The films of Émile Nelligan

155- What are the three key facts about Canada's system of government?

A) Canada is a federal state, a parliamentary democracy and a constitutional monarchy

B) Canada is a British Kingdom, a parliamentary democracy and a constitutional monarchy

C) Canada is a federal democracy, a parliamentary state and a constitutional monarchy

D) Canada is a federal state, a parliamentary monarchy and a constitutional democracy

156- What are the levels of government in Canada?

A) Federal, provincial, territorial and municipal

B) Federal, provincial, and territorial

C) Provincial, territorial and municipal

D) Federal and provincial

157- When were the responsibilities of the federal and provincial governments defined?

A) 1767

B) 1749

C) 1867

D) 1849

158- What is the former name of the Constitution Act?

A) The British North American Act

B) The British Act

C) The Federal Act

D) The French North American Act

159- In which Act are the responsibilities of the federal and provincial governments defined?

A) The Responsibilities Act

B) The Constitution Act

C) The Federal Act

D) The Government Act

160- What is the shared jurisdiction of the federal and provincial governments?

A) Natural Resources and immigration

B) Agriculture and immigration

C) Agriculture and civil rights

D) Education and highways

161- How are senators chosen?

A) They are appointed by the Prime Minister

B) They are appointed by the Governor General on the advice of the Prime Minister

C) They are appointed by the House of Commons

D) They are elected by the people

162- What does "federalism" mean?

A) Canada is a federal country

B) The Federal Government has jurisdiction over certain matters

C) The Federal government has the final decision over all matters

D) The different provinces can adopt policies tailored to their own populations

163- Every province has its own elected Legislative Assembly

A) True

B) False

164-How many territories are there in Canada?

A) Four

B) Three

C) Two

D) One

165- What does "parliamentary democracy" mean?

A) The senators elect members to the House of Commons in Ottawa and to the provincial and territorial legislatures

B) The people elect members to the House of Commons in Ottawa and to the provincial and territorial legislatures

C) The parliament elects members to the House of Commons in Ottawa and to the provincial and territorial legislatures

D) The Queen elects members to the House of Commons in Ottawa and to the provincial and territorial legislatures

166- Which of the following is a responsibility of the members to the House of Commons in
Ottawa and to the provincial and territorial
legislatures?

A) Keeping the government accountable

B) Education and health

C) Matters of international concern

D) Agriculture and immigration

167- What are the responsibilities of the
members to the House of Commons in Ottawa and
to the provincial and territorial legislatures?

A) Passing laws, and approving and monitoring expenditures

B) Passing laws, approving and monitoring
expenditures, and keeping the government
accountable

C) Monitoring expenditures, and keeping the
government accountable

D) Matters of international concern

168- What does it mean to retain the "confidence of the House"?

A) The House of Commons has to have confidence in the Prime Minister

B) The House of Commons has to have confidence in the senators

C) The Queen has to have confidence in the Cabinet ministers

D) Cabinet ministers are responsible to the elected representatives

169- What happens if the cabinet ministers are defeated in a non-confidence vote?

A) They have to resign

B) They keep their positions for one more year only

C) They keep their positions for 6 more months only

D) Nothing

170- What comprises a provincial legislature?

A) The provincial MPs and the elected Assembly

B) The elected Assembly

C) The Lieutenant Governor and the elected Assembly

D) The provincial MPs

171- How does a bill become a law?

A) The bill must be passed by the House of Commons and the Senate, and must receive royal assent

B) The bill must be signed by the Queen or King of England

C) The bill must be approved by the Members of the Parliament

D) The bill must be passed by the House of Commons

172- What are the responsibilities of the federal government?

A) Matters of national and international concern

B) Matters of national concern

C) Matters of international concern

D) Matters of provincial concern

173- Which of the following is the responsibility of federal government?

A) Health

B) Criminal law and citizenship

C) Education

D) Natural Resources

174- For what are the provincial governments responsible?

A) Education, health, and natural resources

B) Natural resources, property, civil rights, and highways

C) Natural resources and highways

D) Education, health, natural resources, property, civil rights, and highways

175- Which of the following is a responsibility of the provinces?

A) Foreign policy

B) Defence

C) Highways

D) Interprovincial trade

176- What does "federalism" do?

A) Gives all the power to the federal government

B) Allows different provinces to adopt policies tailored to their own populations

C) Gives all the power to the Prime Minister

D) Allows the Federal government to adopt policies for all provinces

177- Where are the Parliament buildings located?

A) Ottawa

B) Toronto

C) Vancouver

D) Quebec City

178- In Canada, how are political representatives chosen (members of the House of Commons and members of the provincial and territorial legislatures)?

A) They are elected by the people

B) They are elected by the Senators

C) They are elected by the Prime Minister

D) They are elected by the Cabinet Ministers

179- Which one of the following is not a responsibility of a political representative (members of the House of Commons and members of the provincial and territorial legislatures)?

A) Passing laws

B) Approving and monitoring expenditures

C) Keeping the government accountable

D) Select the Cabinet Ministers

180- What does it mean for the Cabinet Ministers to retain the "confidence of the House"?

A) Cabinet ministers have to resign if they are defeated in a non-confidence vote

B) Cabinet ministers must swear allegiance to the House of England

C) Cabinet ministers must retain the confidence of the people

D) The House of Commons is responsible for the Cabinet ministers

181- What are the three parts of Parliament?

A) Police, Senate and House of Commons

B) Sovereign, Premier and House of Commons

C) Sovereign, Senate and House of Parliament

D) Sovereign, Senate and House of Commons

182- Who selects the Cabinet Ministers?

A) The Prime Minister

B) The Queen

C) The Senators

D) The people of Canada

183- For what is the Prime Minister of Canada responsible?

A) Matters of national concern

B) Education, health, and natural resources

C) The operations and policy of the government

D) The operations of the government

184- What is the "House of Commons"?

A) The representative chamber made up of members of Parliament

B) The representative chamber made up of Senators

C) The representative chamber made up of Cabinet Ministers

D) The representative chamber made up of Federal Deputies

185-How often are members of Parliament elected?

A) Two years

B) Four years

C) Five years

D) Ten years

186- How are Senators appointed?

A) By the Prime Minister

B) By the Queen on the advice of the Prime Minister

C) They are elected by the people

D) By the Governor General on the advice of the Prime Minister

187- Who considers and reviews proposals for new laws?

A) The House of Commons and the Senate

B) The House of Commons

C) The Senate

D) The Cabinet Ministers

188- What is a proposal for a new law called?

A) A new law

B) A law proposal

C) A billCorrect

D) A draft law

189- How can a bill become a law in Canada?

A) It passed by the House of Common and receives royal assent

B) It is passed by both chambers and receives royal assent

C) It passed by Senate and receives royal assent

D) The people vote in favour of the law

190- For a bill to become a law, how many readings must it go through?

A) One

B) Two

C) Three

D) None

191- What form of government does Canada have?

A) Constitutional Monarchy

B) Monarchy

C) Republic

D) Autocracy

192- Who is Canada's Head of State?

   A) The Prime Minister

   B) The Queen

   C) The Senators

   D) The Governor General

193- What is a "hereditary Sovereign"?

   A) A Queen or a King

   B) A Prime Minister

   C) A Governor General

   D) A Senator

194- What does "constitutional monarchy" mean?

   A) The responsibilities of the federal and provincial governments are constitutional

   B) The Sovereign (Queen or King) has the constitutional rights to make laws in Canada

   C) Canada's Head of State is a hereditary Sovereign (Queen or King)

   D) Freedom of speech and mobility

195- How does Canada's Head of State reign?

A) In accordance with the British Constitution only

B) In accordance with the Constitution: the rule of law

C) By making decision alone

D) By directly governing the country

196- What would best describe the role of the Queen in Canada?

A) The Queen is a symbol of Canadian sovereignty and a guardian of constitutional freedoms

B) The Queen must approve all government decisions

C) The Queen appoints all Cabinet Ministers and Prime Ministers

D) The Queen is a symbol of Canadian citizenship and mobility rights

www.toptenaward.org

197- To how many other Commonwealth nations is Canada linked?

A) 12

B) 49

C) 6

D) 53

198- Who is Canada's head of government?

A) The Queen

B) The Prime Minister

C) The House of Commons

D) The people

199- What is the difference between the Head of State and the Head of Government?

A) The Head of Government actually directs the governing of the country

B) The Head of Government doesn't actually direct the governing of the country

C) The Head of State must approve all government decisions

D) The Head of State appoints the Head of Government

200- Who is the Sovereign represented by in Canada?

A) The Governor General

B) The Prime Minister

C) The Lieutenant Governor

D) Nobody

201- How is the Governor General chosen?

A) Appointed by the Sovereign on the advice of the Prime Minister

B) Appointed by the Prime Minister

C) Elected by the people

D) Elected by the House of Commons

202- What do you call the Queen's representative in the provinces?

A) Premier

B) Member of Parliament

C) Senator

D) Lieutenant Governor

203- How is the Lieutenant Governor chosen?

A) Appointed by the Sovereign on the advice of the Prime Minister

B) Appointed by the Prime Minister

C) Appointed by the Governor General

D) Appointed by the Governor General on the advice of the Prime Minister

204- What are the three branches of Canadian government?

A) Executive, Legislative and Monarchy

B) Senate, Legislative and Judicial

C) Executive, Federal and Judicial

D) Executive, Legislative and Judicial

205- What do Canadians vote for in a federal election?

A) The Governor General they want to represent them in Canada

B) The people they want to represent them in the House of Commons

C) A person to become the Premier of Canada

D) All candidates in their electoral district

206- What do the initials "MP" stand for in Canadian politics?

A) Member of Parliament

B) Member of Politics

C) Masters of Parliament

D) Ministers of Parliaments

207- When must federal elections be held?

A) Every four years following the most recent general election

B) Every five years following the most recent general election

C) By order of the Queen

D) By order of the Prime Minister

208- Into how many electoral districts is Canada divided?

A) 196

B) 308

C) 208

D) 402

209- What is an electoral district?

A) The building in which the voting poll is located

B) A geographical area represented by a member of Parliament

C) The area in which elections are held

D) The government office in which you register for voting

210- Who do the citizens in each electoral district elect?

A) Member of Parliament

B) Member of Politics

C) Masters of Parliament

D) Ministers of Parliaments

211- Who has the right to run as a candidate in federal elections?

A) Canadian citizens who are 18 years old or older

B) Canadian citizens and landed immigrants

C) Canadian citizens

D) Canadian citizens who are 16 years or older

212- In Canadian politics, what are the people who run for office called?

A) Electors

C) Politicians

B) Member

D) Candidates

213- How are members of Parliament chosen?

A) They are appointed by the United Nations

B) They are chosen by the provincial Premiers

C) They are elected by voters in their local constituency

D) They are elected by landowners and police chiefs

214- Who does a member of Parliament represent?

A) The citizens in his/her electoral district, as well as all Canadians

B) Only the citizens in his/her electoral district

C) The Provincial and Territorial governments

D) The Provincial Courts

215-What do you call the people who run for office?

A) Electives

B) Officers

C) Candidates

D) Ministers

216- There can be many candidates in an electoral district

A) True

B) False

217-In a federal election, in each electoral district, what does the candidate who receives the most votes become?

A) The MLA

B) The MPC

C) The MPP

D) The MNA

218- How many candidates can there be in an electoral district?

A) Two

B) Three

C) A maximum of five

D) Many

219- Who has the right to vote in a federal election?

A) A Canadian citizen, at least 18 years old on voting day and on the voters' list

B) An adult Canadian citizen

C) Adult Canadian citizens and permanent residents

D) Canadian citizens on the voters' list

220- Which of the following criteria makes you eligible to vote?

A) You own a property in Canada

B) You are on the voters' list

C) You have a valid Canadian driving license

D) You are a landed immigrant

221- Which of the following is not allowed by a non-Canadian Citizen?

A) Vote in a federal or provincial election

B) Own a house

C) Go to University

D) Drive a car

www.toptenaward.org

222-What is the National Register of Electors?

A) A database of Canadian citizens 18 years of age or older who are qualified to vote in federal elections and referendums

B) A database of Canadian citizens 18 years of age or older who are qualified to run as a candidate in federal elections

C) A database of landed immigrants 18 years of age or older who have to register to vote in federal elections and referendums

D) A database of taxpayers who elected to serve on a jury

223- What is the name of the agency that produces the voters' list?

A) Voters Canada

B) Elections Canada

C) Electives Canada

D) Voting Canada

224- How does Elections Canada give the election card to the electors whose names are in the National Register of Electors?

A) Door delivery

B) By mail

C) Electors have to pick it up their voter information card at an Elections Canada's office   D) None of the above

225- What information does the Elector Card contain?

A) When and where to vote

B) The number to call if an interpreter or other special services are required

C) When and where to vote and the number to call if an interpreter or other special services are required

D) The elector's name

226- What happens if you are not listed in the National Register of Electors?

A) You can still be added to the voters' list at any time, including election day

B) You won't be able to vote

C) You can still be added to the voters' list at any time, excluding election day

D) You can still be added to the voters' list but only on election day

227- How do Canadians vote?

A) Online

B) By open ballot

C) By secret ballot   D) By mail

228- What does a vote by secret ballot mean?

A) No one can watch you vote and no one should look at how you voted

B) No one can watch you vote except the election officials

C) You can only show your ballot to one person

D) You must not tell anyone who you voted for

229- Who has the right to insist that you tell them how you voted?

A) Your family members

B) Your union representatives

C) Your employer

D) Nobody

230- How are the results of an election announced in Canada?

A) Announced on radio

B) Announced on radio, on television, and in the newspapers

C) Announced on television

D) Announced in the newspaper

231- After an election, who is invited by the Governor General to form the government?

A) The leader of the political party with the most seats in the House of Commons

B) The leader who has the approval of the Queen

C) The leader who has been directly elected by Canadians

D) The members of Parliament

233- What is the leader of the party with the most seats in the House of Commons called?

A) Queen or King

B) Prime Minister

C) Governor General

D) Senator

www.toptenaward.org

234- What is a majority government?

A) The party in power that holds at least half of the seats in the House of Commons

B) The party in power that holds at least half of the seats in the Senate

C) The party in power that holds at least half of the seats in the Senate and the House of Commons

D) The party in power that holds less than half of the seats in the House of Commons

235- What is a minority government?

A) The party in power that holds less than half of the seats in the Senate

B) The party in power that holds less than half of the seats in the House of Commons

C) The party in power that holds less than half of the seats in the Senate and the House of Commons

D) The party in power that holds at least half of the seats in the House of Commons

www.toptenaward.org

236-The Prime Minister and the party in power run the government:

A) As long as they have the support or confidence of the majority of the MPs

B) As long as they are in good health

C) As long as they have the approval of the Queen

D) As long as they have the support of the senators

237- In Canada, how can a party in power be defeated?

A) If a majority of the members of the House of Commons vote in favor of a major government decision

B) If the Queen votes against a major government decision

C) If a majority of the members of the House of Commons vote against a major government decision

D) If the Governor General resigns

238- What is usually the result of a party in power being defeated?

A) The Governor General asks the Prime Minister, on behalf of the Sovereign, to call an election

B) The Prime Minister must resign from his party

C) The opposition party automatically gets to run the government

D) the Prime Minister asks the Governor General, on behalf of the Sovereign, to call an election

239- Who chooses the ministers of the Crown?

A) The Queen

B) The Prime Minister

C) The Governor General

D) The Senators

240- What is the responsibility of the Cabinet Ministers?

A) They are responsible for running the federal government departments

B) They are responsible for running the Senate

C) They are responsible for running the House of Commons

D) They are responsible for running each province of Canada

241- What forms the Cabinet?

A) The Prime Minister and the Cabinet ministers

B) The Prime Minister and the House of Commons

C) The Prime Minister and the Senators

D) The Senate and the House of Commons

242- Who can question the decisions of the government?

A) The Senate only

B) Only certain members of the House of Commons

C) The Queen only

D) All members of the House of Commons

243- What are the responsibilities of the Cabinet?

A) International matters

B) Natural Resources

C) Prepare the budget and propose most new laws

D) Education

244- What is the opposition party with the most members of the House of Commons called?

A) the Official Opposition or Her Majesty's Loyal Opposition

B) The Outside Opposition or Her Majesty's Loyal Opposition

C) The Side Opposition

D) The Loyal Great Opposition

245- What is the name of the parties that are not in power?

A) Outside parties

B) Side parties

C) Powerless parties   D) Opposition parties

246- What is the role of opposition parties?

A) To peacefully oppose or try to improve government proposals

B) To help the Prime Minister

C) To approve the leader party's bills

D) To write bills

247- What are the names of the three major political parties currently represented in the House of Commons?

A) Conservative Party, Liberal Party and New Royal Party

B) Conservative Party, Liberal Party and New Democratic Party

C) Quebec Coalition, Conservative Party and Liberal Party

D) New Democratic Party, Royal Party, and French Coalition

248- What is a voter information card?

A) A card that confirms that your name is on the voters' list and states when and where you vote

B) A card that you use to register for voting

C) A letter explaining how to vote

D) A list with all the election candidates

249- Who will receive a voter information card?

A) Electors who own a house

B) Everybody

C) Electors whose information is in the National Register of Electors

D) Electors who are 18 years or older

250- During an election period, what happens if you do not receive a voter information card?

A) You cannot vote

B) You can only vote online

C) You have to call the House of Commons in Ottawa to ensure that you are on the voters' list

D) You have to call your local elections office, or Elections Canada in Ottawa, to ensure that you are on the voters' list

www.toptenaward.org

251- What happens if you cannot or do not wish to vote on election day?

A) You can vote at the advance polls only

B) You can vote at the advance polls or by special ballot

C) You can vote by special ballot only

D) You cannot vote at all

252-What should you do on election day?

A) Go to your polling station

B) Nothing

C) Go to the nearest Election Canada's office

D) Call Elections Canada

253- On election day, what should you bring to the polling station?

A) The voter information card and proof of your identity and address

B) The voter information card

C) A piece of identification

D) Nothing

254- During an election period, where is the location of your polling station indicated?

A) In your local Member of Parliament's office

B) On your ballot

C) On your voter information card

D) Online

255- What do you mark on a federal election ballot?

A) An "X"

B) The candidate's name

C) The candidate's number

D) The party's name

www.toptenaward.org

256- In the Canadian justice system, what is the "presumption of innocence"?

A) Everyone is guilty until proven innocent

B) Everyone is innocent until proven guilty

C) Everyone is innocent until proven innocent

D) Everyone is guilty until proven guilty

257- In the Canadian justice system, what is "due process"?

A) The principle that the government must respect all of legal rights a person is entitled to under the law

B) The principle that the government must respect certain legal rights a person is entitled under the law

C) The principle that the government must complete a particular judicial process before convicting anyone

D) The principle that the government has its own process when dealing with criminals

258- In Canada, how are the rules made?

A) By the people

B) By the Queen

C) By the Prime Minister

D) By elected representatives

259- In Canada, to which following category do the laws not apply?

A) Judges

B) Politicians

C) Police

D) None of the above

260- Which of the following is not an objective of the laws in Canada?

A) Provide order in society

B) Provide a peaceful way to settle disputes

C) Put more people in jail

D) Express the values and beliefs of Canadians

261- What does the Federal Court deal with?

A) Matters concerning the federal government

B) Matters concerning the federal and provincial government

C) Matters concerning the police

D) Matters concerning National Defence

262- In Canada, the police are there to help you.

A) True

B) False

263- What is the role of the police in Canada?

A) To resolve legal disputes

B) To defend Canadian borders

C) To keep people safe and to enforce the lawC

D) To provide National Security data to the Federal government

264- In which of the following situations can you not ask the police for help?

A) There has been an accident

B) Someone has stolen something from you

C) You are a victim of assault

D) Your water pipes are leaking

265- Which of the following is not a responsibility of the RCMP in Canada?

A) Enforce federal laws throughout Canada

B) Serve as municipal police in all major
cities in Canada

C) Serve as the provincial police in all
provinces and territories except Ontario
and Quebec

D) Serve as the provincial police in some
municipalities

266- In which province(s) does the RCMP not
serve as the provincial police?

A) Ontario

B) Quebec

C) Ontario and Quebec

D) Manitoba and Alberta

267- In Canada, you can question the police
about their service or conduct if you feel
the need.

A) True

B) False

268- Which one of the following is not a provincial court?

A) Court of Queen's Bench

B) Small claims court

C) Traffic court

D) High court

269- Since when have red and white been the national colors of Canada?

A) 1965

B) 1949

C) 1921

D) 1892

270- When was the maple leaf first adopted as a symbol in Canada?

A) In the 1700s

B) In the 1800s

C) In the 1600s

D) In the 1900s

271- When was "O Canada" proclaimed as the national anthem?

A) 1867

B) 1889

C) 1980

D) 1947

272- What year did Canada start its own honours system?

A) 1867

B) 1889

C) 1967

D) 1947

273- When do Canadians celebrate Victoria Day?

A) Tuesday preceding May 25th

B) Monday preceding June 25th

C) Monday preceding May 25th

D) Tuesday preceding June 25th

274- When do Canadians celebrate Remembrance Day?

A) November 11th

B) November 21st

C) October 11th

D) September 11th

275- What is the NAFTA agreement?

A) Free trade between Canada, the United States and Mexico

B) Free trade between Canada, the United States and Europe

C) Free trade between Canada, the United States and the United Kingdom

D) Free trade between Canada, the Europe and Mexico

276- Canada's economy is among the top:

A) 5

B) 10

C) 20

D) 3

277- In what area do Canadians mostly work nowadays?

A) Manufacturing industries

B) Natural resources industries

C) Farming industries

D) Service Industries

278- Which industries have played an important part in Canada's story and development?

A) Manufacturing industries

B) Service industries

C) Natural resources industries

D) Trading industries

279- Who is Canada's largest international trading partner?

A) United States

B) Mexico

C) Europe

D) China

280- What is traditionally known as "the world's longest undefended border"?

A) Both Canadian Atlantic and Pacific coasts

B) Mexico-U.S.A border

C) Canada-U.S.A border

D) The Great Wall of China

281- Which of the following statements is false about the Canada-U.S.A. relationship?

A) They have the biggest bilateral trading relationship in the world

B) Canada exports almost no goods to the U.S.A.

C) They have the world's longest undefended border

D) Millions of Canadians and Americans cross every year the Canada-U.S.A. border

282- hich following countries are part of the G8?

A) United States, Germany, the United Kingdom, Italy, France, Canada, China and Russia

B) United States, Germany, the United Kingdom, Japan, Canada, Russia, France and China

C) United States, the United Kingdom, Japan, Canada, Australia, Russia, France and China

D) United States, Germany, the United Kingdom, Italy, France, Japan, Canada and Russia

www.toptenaward.org

283- To which industries do transportation, education, health care, construction, banking, communications, retail services, tourism and government belong to?

A) Manufacturing industries

B) Natural resources industries

C) Service industries

D) Trading Industries

284- To which industries do products such as paper, high technology equipment, aerospace technology, automobiles, machinery, food and clothing belong to?

A) Service industries

B) Manufacturing industries

C) Natural resources industries

D) Trading Industries

285- To which industries do forestry, fishing, agriculture, mining and energy belong to?

A) Service industries

B) Manufacturing industries

C) Trading Industries

D) Natural resources industries

286- What are the regions of Canada?

A) Atlantic Provinces, Central Canada, Prairie Provinces, West Coast and Northern Territories

B) South Provinces, Northern Canada, West Provinces, East Provinces, and Central Territories

C) Ontario, Quebec, Prairie Provinces and Central Canada

D) Atlantic Provinces, Central Canada, Prairie Provinces, and West Coast

287- Who chose Ottawa as the capital of Canada?

A) Queen Elizabeth II

B) Queen Elizabeth I

C) Queen Anne

D) Queen Victoria

www.toptenaward.org

288- Which of the following are Atlantic Provinces?

A) Ontario, Nova Scotia, New Brunswick and Labrador

B) Newfoundland, Nova Scotia, New Brunswick and Quebec

C) Newfoundland and Labrador, Prince Edward Island, New Brunswick and Quebec

D) Newfoundland and Labrador, Nova Scotia, New Brunswick and Prince Edward Island

289- Which of the following is a West Coast Province?

A) Nunavut

B) Nova Scotia

C) British Columbia   D) Alberta

290- Which of the following defines Northern Canada?

A) Nunavut, Northwest Territories and Yukon

B) Nunavut and Northwest Territories

C) Northwest Territories and Yukon

D) Nunavut, Northwest Territories and New-foundland

291- What is the capital of Nova Scotia?

A) Charlottetown

B) St. John's

C) Fredericton

D) Halifax

292- What is the capital of New Brunswick?

A) Halifax

B) Fredericton

C) Winnipeg

D) Regina

293- What is the capital of Ontario?

A) Ottawa

B) Toronto

C) Kingston

D) Mississauga

294- What is the capital of Manitoba?

A) Regina

B) Edmonton

C) Winnipeg

D) Calgary

295- What is the capital of British Columbia?

A) Vancouver

B) Victoria

C) Calgary

D) Edmonton

296- What is the capital of Nunavut?

A) Yellowknife

B) Inuit

C) Edmonton

D) Iqaluit

595 CANADIAN CITIZENSHIP TESTS • 111

297- What is the capital of the Northwest Territories?

A) Whitehorse

B) Edmonton

C) Yellowknife

D) Iqaluit

298- Which of the following does not border Alberta?

A) British Columbia

B) Manitoba

C) Saskatchewan

D) Northwest Territories

299- Which of the following does not border the Yukon?

A) Arctic Ocean

B) Northwest Territories

C) British Columbia

D) Alberta

300- Which of the following does not border Nunavut?

A) Arctic Ocean

B) Northwest Territories

C) Manitoba

D) Ontario

301- Which of the following does not border Saskatchewan?

A) U.S.A.

B) Alberta

C) Manitoba

D) British Columbia

302- Which of the following does not border Manitoba?

A) Quebec

B) Saskatchewan

C) Ontario

D) U.S.A.

303- Which of the following does not border Ontario?

A) Nova Scotia

B) Manitoba

C) Quebec

D) Hudson Bay

304- Which of the following does not border Quebec?

A) Ontario

B) New Brunswick

C) Nova Scotia

D) Atlantic Ocean

305- Which of the following borders Nova Scotia?

A) New Brunswick

B) Quebec

C) Prince Edward Island

D) Ontario

306- Which of the following provinces/territories borders the Pacific Ocean?

A) Quebec

B) British Columbia

C) Northwest Territories

D) Alberta

307- Which of the following provinces/territories does not border the U.S.A.?

A) Quebec

B) British Columbia

C) Nunavut

D) Alberta

308- Which of the following provinces/territories borders with the Atlantic Ocean?

A) Newfoundland and Labrador

B) British Columbia

C) Saskatchewan

D) Alberta

309- What is the most easterly point in North America?

A) Prince Edward Island

B) Nova Scotia

C) New Brunswick

D) Newfoundland and Labrador

310- Which province has its own time zone?

A) Nunavut

B) Yukon

C) Newfoundland and Labrador

D) Prince Edward Island

311- What is the oldest colony of the British Empire?

A) Prince Edward Island

B) Newfoundland and Labrador

C) Nova Scotia

D) New Brunswick

312- Which province has long been known for its fisheries, coastal fishing villages and distinct culture?

A) Newfoundland and Labrador

B) Nova Scotia

C) New Brunswick

D) British Columbia

313- What does P.E.I. stand for?

A) Prince Edward Island

B) Prince Edmond Island

C) Port Edward Island

D) Prince Edgar Island

314- What is Canada's smallest province?

A) Nunavut

B) Prince Edward Island

C) Saskatchewan

D) Nova Scotia

315- What is known as the birthplace of Confederation?

A) Ontario

B) Quebec

C) Nova Scotia

D) Prince Edward Island

316- In Canada, where can you find one of the longest continuous multispan bridges in the world?

A) Prince Edward Island

B) Quebec

C) Nova Scotia

D) Ontario

317- In Canada, where can you find Celtic and Gaelic traditions?

A) Newfoundland and Labrador

B) Saskatchewan

C) Nova Scotia

D) Prince Edward Island

318-Where is Canada's largest naval base?

A) Nova Scotia

B) Vancouver

C) New Brunswick

D) Ontario

319- Where is Canada's largest east coast port?

A) Charlottetown

B) St. John's

C) Halifax

D) Fredericton

320- In Canada, where can you find the world's highest tides?

A) Prince Edward Island

B) Quebec

C) Nova Scotia

D) British Columbia

321- Which province has the second largest river system on North America's Atlantic coastline?

A) Quebec

B) Nova Scotia

C) New Brunswick

D) Newfoundland and Labrador

322- Which city is the principal Francophone Acadian centre in Canada?

A) Moncton

B) Quebec City

C) Montreal

D) Charlottetown

323- Which province is the only officially bilingual province?

A) Quebec

B) New Brunswick

C) Nova Scotia

D) Ontario

324- In Canada, where do more than half of the people live?

A) Central Canada

B) Atlantic provinces

C) Prairie provinces

D) West Coast

325- What is known as Canada's industrial and manufacturing heartland?

A) Ontario

B) Alberta

C) Quebec

D) Southern Ontario and Quebec

326- Where are more than three quarters of all Canadian manufactured goods produced?

A) Quebec

B) Ontario

C) Quebec and Ontario

D) Ontario and Manitoba

327- In Quebec, where do the vast majority of people live?

A) Along or near the St. Lawrence River

B) On the Atlantic Coast

C) At the border with Ontario

D) At the border with the U.S.A.

328- In Quebec, how many people speak French as their first language?

A) Less than half

B) About one-third

C) More than three-quarters

D) 100%

329- Which province is Canada's main producer of pulp and paper?

A) New Brunswick

B) Ontario

C) British Columbia

D) Quebec

330- Which province is Canada's largest producer of hydroelectricity?

A) Ontario

B) Quebec

C) British Columbia

D) Manitoba

331- What is "La Francophonie"?

A) A traditional French music

B) A region in Quebec

C) A French-Canadian political party

D) An association of French-speaking nations

332- Which of the following is Canada's second largest city?

A) Toronto

B) Vancouver

C) Montreal

D) Ottawa

333- What is Canada's second largest, mainly French-speaking city in the world, after Paris?

A) Quebec City

B) Montreal

C) Ottawa

D) Halifax

334- Where do one-third of Canadians live?

A) British Colombia

B) Quebec

C) Nova Scotia

D) Ontario

335-Which of the following is Canada's main financial centre and largest city?

A) Toronto

B) Vancouver

C) Montreal

D) Ottawa

336- What three industries are important to Nova Scotia's economy today?

   A) Fisheries, shipbuilding and forestry.

   B) Forestry, mining and tourism.

   C) Coal mining, forestry and agriculture.

   D) Tourism, movies and shipbuilding.

337- How many Canadians have been awarded the Victoria Cross (V.C.), the highest honour available to Canadians?

   A) 56.

   B) 96.

   C) 1,024.

   D) 42.

338- What are the three parts of Parliament?

   A) The Sovereign, Governor General and Prime Minister.

   B) The House of Commons, the Legislative Assembly and the Senate.

   C) The Queen, the Legislative Assembly and the Senate.

   D) The Queen, the House of Commons and the Senate.

595 CANADIAN CITIZENSHIP TESTS • 125

339- What year was Confederation?

    A) 1867.

    B) 1871.

    C) 1898.

    D) 1870.

340- Which provinces first formed Confederation?

  A) Ontario, Quebec, Nova Scotia and Newfoundland.

  B) Ontario, Nova Scotia, New Brunswick and Alberta.

  C) Ontario, Quebec, Prince Edward Island and Nova Scotia.

  D) Nova Scotia, New Brunswick and the Province of Canada.

341- From where does the name "Canada" come?

  A) From the Inuit word meaning country.

  B) From the French word meaning joining.

  C) From the Metis word meaning rivers.

  D) From the Huron-Iroquois word for village.

342- Who was Sir Sam Steele?

   A) A great frontier hero, Mounted Police-
      man and soldier of the Queen.

   B) A great frontier hero, Mounted Police-
      man and a military leader of the Metis
      in the 19th century.

   C) A great frontier hero, Mounted Police-
      man and third Prime Minister of Canada.

   D) A great frontier hero, Mounted Police-
      man and the Father of Manitoba.

www.toptenaward.org

343- When does a federal election have to be
held under legislation passed by Parliament?

   A) Within 5 years of the last election.

   B) The Prime Minister can call the election
      any time at his own will.

   C) Within 4 years of the most recent elec-
      tion.

   D) When the Queen wants to replace the
      Prime Minister.

344-Which of the following are the responsibilities of federal government?

A) National defense, foreign policy, international trade and aboriginal affairs.

B) Education, foreign policy, recycling programs and aboriginal affairs.

C) National defense, health care, international trade and aboriginal affairs.

D) Highways, policing, international trade and criminal justice.

345- For how long did the Hudson Bay Company control the northern lands?

A) 220 years.

B) 180 years.

C) 150 years.   D) 300 years.

346- What are the main functions of the Cabinet?

A) Natural resources

B) Defense

C) Navigation

D) Prepare the budget and propose new laws to implement

347- What does it mean to say that Canada is a constitutional monarchy?

A) The sovereign (queen or king) is the legislator of Canada.

B) The Head of State of Canada is a hereditary sovereign (queen or king) who reigns according to the Constitution.

C) The sovereign (queen or king) approves the law projects before their final adoption.

D) Le souverain (reine ou roi) représente les Canadiens au Parlement.

348- What are the three parts of the Canadian Parliament?

A) Prime Minister, House of Commons and Senate

B) The Prime Minister, the Prime Ministers and the House of Commons

C) The King, The Governor General and the Prime Minister

D) The King, The House of Commons and the Senate

349- What part of the Constitution legally protects the fundamental rights and freedoms of all Canadians?

A) The Canadian Charter of Rights and Freedoms

B) The Canadian Charter of Freedoms

C) The Canadian Charter of Rights

D) The British Charter of Rights and Freedoms

350- What is the name of the Canadian system of political governance?

A) The benevolent dictatorship

B) The democratic process

C) The monarchy

D) The parliamentary government

351- Who has the primary responsibilities on First Nations reserves?

A) Municipal governments.

B) Band leaders and councilors.

C) Provincial and territorial governments.

D) The federal government.

352- Which of the following statements is the responsibility of the provinces?

A) Inter provincial Trade and Communications

B) The municipal administration

C) Currency

D) Navigation

353- Which of the following statements is a key phrase in the British North America Act, the original constitutional document of Canada in 1867?

A) Peace, Order and Good Governance

B) A geopolitical entity

C) Discipline, education and the public good

D) Trade and communications

354- What is the highest court in Canada?

A) Supreme Court of Canada

B) The King's Court

C) The Assize Court of Canada

D) The Senate Court of Canada

355- For how many years is the Lieutenant Governor appointed?

A) 5 years

B) 4 years

C) 6 years

D) 3 years

356- Who appoints the judges of the Supreme Court of Canada?

A) The Prime Minister

B) The sovereign

C) Commissioner

D) Governor General

357- Which country is Canada's largest trading partner?

A) Japan

B) United States of America

C) China

D) Mexico

358- Which of the following is above the law in Canada?

A) The judges

B) The politicians

C) No one

D) The police

359- What are the three NAFTA countries?

A) Canada, the United Kingdom and the United States.

B) Canada, Denmark and Andorra.

C) Canada, Mexico and the United States.

D) Canada, the United States and Japan.

360- Who is Canada's head of state?

A) The Prime Minister

B) The lieutenant governor

C) His Majesty king charles III

D) Governor General of Canada

361- A Member of Parliament from Montreal announces that she will spend her weekend in her electoral district. This means she would be:

A) In her office on Parliament Hill.

B) Visiting the province of Quebec.

C) In the part of Montreal where she was elected.

D) Going on a vacation.

362- After a federal election, which party forms the new government?

A) The party with the most elected representatives is invited by the Governor General to become the party in power.

B) The King himself picks any party to run the government.

C) The Governor General proposes a law for elected officials to become the governing body.

D) The Premiers of each province pick a party to run the government

363- Approximately how many Canadians served in the First World War?

A) 7000.

B) 8 million.

C) About 60,000.

D) More than 600,000.

364- Canada has three territories and how many provinces?

A) 13

B) 10

C) 3

D) 5

365- Fatima is a new immigrant in Canada. What law allows her to take a job at par with a man?

A) Equality of women and men

B) Equality of all races.

C) Equal pay for equal work.

D) Equal rights.

366- From where does the name "Canada" come from?

A) From the Inuit word meaning country.

B) From the French word meaning joining.

C) From the Métis word meaning rivers.

D) From "Kanata", the Huron-Iroquois word for village.

367- Give an example of how you can show responsibility by participating in your community.

A) Mind your own business.

B) Have a party.

C) Keep your property tidy.

D) Volunteer.

368- Give an example of where English and French have equal status in Canada.

A) In schools.

B) In the workplace.

C) In the Parliament of Canada.

D) At City Hall.

369- Give the first line of Canada's national anthem?

   A) Canada! Our home and native land!

   B) Canada! Our province and native land!

   C) Canada! From far and wide, O Canada,

   D) Canada! We stand on guard for thee.

370- How are Members of Parliament chosen?

   A) Appointed by the Prime Minister.

   B) Elected by Canadian citizens.

   C) Appointed by the King.

   D) Elected by the Provincial Ministers.

371- How are Senators chosen?

   A) By the Governor General of Canada.

   B) By the Premiers of all provinces.

   C) Appointed by the King.

   D) Senators are appointed by the Governor General on the advice of the Prime Minister.

372- How does a bill become a law?

A) The Lieutenant Governor must approve the bill.

B) Approval by a majority in the House of Commons and Senate and finally the Governor General.

C) The King must sign the bill.

D) Approval by the Members of the Legislative Assembly.

373- How is a Cabinet Minister chosen?

A) By the King.

B) By the voters.

C) By other Cabinet Ministers.

D) By the Prime Minister

374- How is the government formed after a federal election?

   A) The party with the most elected represen-
      tatives becomes the party in power. The
      King chooses the Prime Minister from this
      party

   B) Ordinarily, the party with the most
      elected representatives becomes the par-
      ty in power. The leader of this party
      becomes the Prime Minister.

   C) The Governor General picks a party and a
      Prime Minister to run the government.

   D) Each province elects one representative
      to form the government. The King then
      chooses the Prime Minister.

375-How is the Prime Minister chosen?

   A) The King appoints the Prime Minister.

   B) The Governor General with the Senate ap-
      point the Prime Minister.

   C) The leader of the party with the most
      elected representatives becomes the
      Prime Minister.

   D) The MPs vote on the Prime Minister.

376- In Canada, are you allowed to question the police about their service or conduct?

A) No, police service and conduct is not open to discussion with Canadians.

B) Yes, you can question their service but not their conduct.

C) Yes, you can question their conduct but not their service.

D) Yes, if you feel the need to.

377- In Canada's justice system what does "presumption of innocence" mean?

A) Everyone is guilty until proven innocent

B) Guilt is decided by public opinion

C) Innocence is decided by public opinion

D) Everyone is innocent until proven guilty

378- In the 1960s, Quebec experienced an era of rapid change. What is this called?

A) The West Movement.

B) The Revolution.

C) The Quiet Revolution.

D) La Francophonie.

379- In what industry do most Canadians work?

A) Natural resources

B) Tourism.

C) Service.

D) Manufacturing.

380- In which region do more than half the people in Canada live?

A) Central Canada.

B) Prairies.

C) Atlantic Canada.

D) Northern Canada.

381- Name all the federal political parties in the House of Commons and their leaders

A) Conservative (Poilievre), NDP (Singh), Liberal (Trudeau), Bloc Quebecois (Blanchet), Green Party (Kuttner))

B) Conservative (Scheer), Green (May), Liberal (Trudeau), Bloc Quebecois (Duceppe)

C) NDP (Mulcair), Green (May), Liberal (Rae), Bloc Quebecois (Paillé)

D) Liberal (Ignatieff), Conservative (Ambrose), NDP (Turmel), Green (May)

382- Name six responsibilities of citizenship.

A) Getting a job, making money, raising a
family, paying taxes, mowing your lawn,
voting in provincial elections.

B) Voting in municipal elections only,
joining a political party, getting a
job, obeying the law, driving safely,
picking up litter.

C) Caring for the environment, not lit-
tering, paying taxes, obeying the law,
helping others, respecting others.

D) Obeying the law, taking responsibility
for oneself and one's family, helping
others in the community, voting in elections, serving on a jury, protecting and
enjoying our heritage and environment.

383- Name the five regions of Canada

A) Midwest, North, South, East, Central

B) Maritimes, Ontario, Quebec, Prairies,
and British Columbia

C) Atlantic, Central, Prairie, West Coast,
and North

D) West, Central, East, Prairies, and Territories

384- Name three additional rights protected by the Canadian Charter of Rights and Freedoms

- A) Freedom of speech, Right to own land, and Right to a fair trial.

- B) Mobility rights, Multiculturalism, and Aboriginal Peoples' rights.

- C) Right to ski anywhere in Canada, Moving rights, and Right to public assembly.

- D) Right to vote, Right to speak publicly, and Security rights.

www.toptenaward.org

385- Name two fundamental freedoms protected by the Canadian Charter of Rights and Freedoms.

- A) Freedom of conscience and religion, and Freedom of association.

- B) Equality rights, and to care for Canada's heritage.

- C) Basic freedoms, and obeying laws.

- D) Aboriginal peoples' rights, and to volunteer.

386- Name two key documents that contain our rights and freedoms.

A) The Canadian Constitution and English common law.

B) Civil code of France and the Canadian Constitution.

C) Canadian Charter of Rights and Freedoms and Magna Carta (the Great Charter of Freedoms).

D) Laws passed by Parliament and English common law.

387- Name two responsibilities of the federal government.

A) National defence and firefighting.

B) National defence and foreign policy.

C) Citizenship and highways.

D) Recycling and education.

388- Name two responsibilities of the provincial and territorial government.

   A) Citizenship and Foreign Policy

   B) Health and Education

   C) Defense and Currency

   D) Criminal Law and Interprovincial Trade

389- On what date did Nunavut become a territory?

   A) July 1st, 1867

   B) April 1st, 1999

   C) June 24th, 1995

   D) March 31st, 1949

390- One third of all Canadians live in which province?

   A) Quebec.

   B) Ontario.

   C) Northwest Territories.

   D) Manitoba.

391- The Canadian Coat of Arms and motto is "A Mari Usque Ad Mare." This means:

A) From the ocean to the sea.

B) From sea to sea.

C) From the sea to the ends of the earth.

D) From the water to the earth.

392- What are some examples of taking responsibility for yourself and your family?

A) Buying a house and a TV.

B) Getting a job, taking care of one's family and working hard in keeping with one's abilities.

C) Doing laundry and keeping the house clean.

D) Study hard so you can earn enough money to take a vacation.

393- What are the Prairie provinces and their capital cities?

A) Alberta (Edmonton) and Saskatchewan (Regina).

B) Alberta (Edmonton), Saskatchewan (Regina) and Manitoba (Winnipeg).

C) Saskatchewan (Regina) and Manitoba (Winnipeg).

D) Saskatchewan (Regina), Manitoba (Winnipeg) and Ontario (Toronto).

www.toptenaward.org

394- What are the provinces of Central Canada and their capital cities?

A) Manitoba (Winnipeg) and Ontario (Toronto).

B) Quebec (Quebec City) and Prince Edward Island (Charlottetown).

C) Ontario (Toronto) and Quebec (Quebec City).

D) Saskatchewan (Regina) and Manitoba Winnipeg).

595 CANADIAN CITIZENSHIP TESTS • 147

395- What are the provinces of the Atlantic region and their capital cities?

A) Nova Scotia (Halifax), New Brunswick (Fredericton), Prince Edward Island (Charlottetown) and Quebec (Quebec).

B) Newfoundland and Labrador (St. John's), Nova Scotia (Halifax), New Brunswick (Fredericton) and Prince Edward Island (Charlottetown).

C) Newfoundland and Labrador (St. John's), Nova Scotia (Halifax), New Brunswick (Fredericton) and Quebec (Quebec).

D) Nova Scotia (Halifax), New Brunswick (Fredericton), Quebec (Quebec City)and Ontario (Toronto).

396- What are the territories of Northern Canada and their capital cities?

A) Alaska (Juneau) and Yukon Territory (Whitehorse).

B) Northwest Territories (Yellowknife) and Alaska (Juneau).

C) Northwest Territories (Yellowknife).

D) Yukon Territory (Whitehorse), Northwest Territories (Yellowknife), and Nunavut (Iqaluit).

397- What are the three levels of government in Canada?

A) Federal, Provincial and Territorial, Municipal (local).

B) Federal, Provincial and City.

C) Federal, Territorial and Provincial.

D) Federal, State and Local.

398- What are the three main groups of Aboriginal peoples?

A) First Nations, Métis and Inuit.

B) Acadians, Métis and Inuit.

C) United Empire Loyalists, Métis and Inuit.

D) Inuit, Métis and Acadians.

399- What are the three main types of industry in Canada?

A) Natural resources, tourism and service industries..

B) Tourism, services and manufacturing.

C) Natural resources, tourism and manufacturing.

D) Natural resources, manufacturing and services.

400- What are the three parts of Parliament?

A) The Sovereign, Governor General and Prime Minister.

B) The House of Commons, the Legislative Assembly and the Senate.

C) The King, the Legislative Assembly and the Senate.

D) The Sovereign, the House of Commons and the Senate.

401- What are the two official languages of Canada?

A) English and Métis.

B) Inuktitut and French.

C) English and French.

D) English and Inuktitut.

402- What country is Canada's largest trading partner?

A) Mexico.

B) United States of America.

C) China.

D) Japan.

403- What did the Canadian Pacific Railway symbolize?

A) Easy access to the West Coast.

B) What can be achieved by working together.

C) Unity.

D) Ribbons of steel.

404- What did the Fathers of Confederation do?

A) They worked together to establish a new country, the Dominion of Canada

B) They were explorers who formed an expedition to survey Northern Canada

C) They formed a republic state in Canada

D) They were a group of politicians that tried to unite Canada to the United States

405- What do you call a law before it is passed?

A) A New law.

B) A Proposed law.

C) A Bill.

D) A New proposal.

406- What do you call the Sovereign's representative in the provinces?

A) Premier.

B) Member of the Legislative Assembly.

C) Lieutenant-Governor.

D) Senator.

407- What do you mark on a federal election ballot?

A) The candidate's name.

B) The number for the candidate.

C) An "X".

D) The voter's name.

408- What does Confederation mean?

A) The United States Confederate soldiers came to Canada.

B) Joining of communities to become a province.

C) Joining of suburbs to form a large city.

D) Joining of provinces to make a new country.

409- What does it mean to say Canada is a constitutional monarchy?

A) The Sovereign (Queen or King) is the law maker of Canada.

B) Canada's Head of State is a hereditary Sovereign (Queen or King) who reigns in accordance with the Constitution.

C) The Sovereign (Queen or King) represents Canadians in Parliament.

D) The Sovereign (Queen or King) approves bills before becoming law.

410- What does the "right to a secret ballot" mean?

A) No one should tell you where to vote

B) A secret vote used by politicians when they are voting on sensitive topics

C) No one can watch your vote and no one should look at how you voted

D) Your right to vote in secret on who to appoint to the Senate

411- What does the Canadian flag look like?

A) Red and white with provincial emblems.

B) Red and white with a beaver.

C) White with a red border on each end and a red maple leaf in the centre.

D) Red with a white maple leaf.

412- What does the term "responsible government" mean?

A) Each person in each electoral district is
responsible for voting.

B) The Governor General is responsible for
the actions of the Prime Minister.

C) The ministers of the Crown must have the
support of a majority of the elected
representatives in order to govern.

D) All Canadians are responsible for each
other.

413- What does the word "Inuit" mean?

A) "Eskimo" in Inuktitut language.

B) "Home" in English.

C) "The people" in the Inuktitut language.

D) "The Arctic Land" in Inuktitut language.

414- What happened at the Battle of the Plains of Abraham?

A) The Voyagers battled with the British for fur trading rights

B) Americans fought the United Empire Loyalists during the American Revolution

C) The British defeated the French marking the end of France's empire in America

D) The French defeated the British in a battle for Quebec

www.toptenaward.org

415- What is a Francophone?

A) A person who speaks English as their first language

B) A smartphone designed by the Canadian company RIM

C) A person who speaks French as their first language

D) The first phone in Canada, invented by Alexander Graham Bell

416- What is a major river in Quebec?

A) Fraser River

B) St. Lawrence River

C) Niagara

D) Hudson's Bay.

www.toptenaward.org

417- What is a majority government?

A) When the party in power holds about one third of the seats in the House of Commons

B) When the party in power holds about one quarter of the seats in the House of Commons.

C) When the part in power holds at least half of the seats in the Senate.

D) When the party in power holds at least half of the seats in the House of Commons.

418- What is a voter information card?

A) Tells you who the candidates are in your electoral district.

B) Tells you what province to vote in.

C) A form that tells you when and where to vote.

D) A form that lets you know your voting time.

419- What is Canada's national winter sport?

A) Golf.

B) Nordic skiing.

C) Lacrosse.

D) Hockey.

420- What is Canada's system of government called?

A) Dictatorship.

B) Parliamentary government.

C) Military Rule.

D) Communism.

421- What is meant by the equality of women and men?

   A) Men and women are equal under the law.

   B) Men and women must both do housework.

   C) Women may now go to school and enter the professional workforce.

   D) A woman may now become Prime Minister.

422- What is the "head tax"?

   A) Race-based entry fee charged for Chinese entering Canada.

   B) Fee charged for anyone entering Canada after 1900.

   C) A tax imposed on beer beginning in 1867.

   D) Fee charged for moving westward in the early 1900s.

423- What is the capital city of Canada?

   A) Ottawa.

   B) Toronto.

   C) Montreal.

   D) Hull.

424- What is the difference between the role of the Sovereign and that of the Prime Minister?

A) The Sovereign is Head of State, the Prime Minister oversees provincial policies.

B) The Sovereign is the guardian of Constitutional freedoms, the Prime Minister selects the Cabinet ministers and is responsible for operations and policy of government.

C) The Sovereign links Canada to 52 other nations and the Prime Minister is the guardian of Constitutional freedoms.

D) The Sovereign is the symbol of Canadian sovereignty and the Prime Minister is her aide.

425- What is the government of all of Canada called?

A) National assembly.

B) Legislature.

C) Federal.

D) Council.

426- What is the highest court in Canada?

A) The Queen's Court

B) The Senate Court of Canada

C) The Supreme Court of Canada

D) The Crown Court of Canada

427- What is the highest military honour a Canadian can receive?

A) Purple Cross.

B) Badge of Courage.

C) Order of Merit.

D) Victoria Cross.

428- What is the largest religious affiliation in Canada?

A) Catholic.

B) Muslim.

C) Jewish.

D) Hindu.

429- What is the meaning of the Remembrance Day poppy?

   A) To remember our Sovereign, Queen Elizabeth II.

   B) To celebrate Confederation.

   C) To honour Prime Ministers who have died.

   D) To remember the sacrifice of Canadians who have served or died in wars up to the present day.

430- What is the name of the Governor General?

   A) David Johnston.

   B) Mary Simon.

   C) Richard Wagner.

   D) Julie Payette

431- What is the name of the Prime Minister of Canada and his/her party?

   A) Justin Trudeau (Liberal Party).

   B) Andrew Scheer (Conservative Party).

   C) Jagmeet Singh (New Democratic Party).

   D) Pierre Trudeau (Liberal Party).

432- What is the name of the Royal Anthem of Canada?

A) Canada.

B) God Save the Queen (or King).

C) La Marseillaise

D) The Star-Spangled Banner.

433- What is the role of the courts in Canada?

A) To enforce the law.

B) To guide people in our society.

C) To settle disputes.

D) To express values and beliefs of Canadians.

434- What is the role of the Opposition parties?

A) To assist the Prime Minister.

B) To sign bills.

C) To oppose or try to improve government proposals.

D) To put forward bills to be passed.

435- What is the significance of the discovery of insulin by Sir Frederick Banting and Charles Best?

A) Insulin is a hormone that permits you to eat anything you wish.

B) Insulin has saved 16 million lives worldwide.

C) Discovering insulin opened the doors to more discoveries.

D) Discovering insulin made Drs. Banting and Best famous.

www.toptenaward.org

436- What part of the Constitution legally protects the basic rights and freedoms of all Canadians?

A) The British Charter of Rights and Freedoms.

B) The Canadian Charter of Rights.

C) The Canadian Charter of Freedoms.

D) The Canadian Charter of Rights and Freedoms.

437- What percentage of Aboriginal people are First Nations?

A) 30%.

B) 6%.

C) 50%.

D) 65%.

438- What should you do if you do not receive a voter information card telling you when and where to vote?

A) Go to the police station.

B) Call your Member of Parliament.

C) Assume you cannot vote.

D) Call Elections Canada or visit their website.

439- What song is Canada's national anthem?

A) God Save the King.

B) Canada.

C) Star Spangled Banner.

D) Amazing Grace.

440- What three oceans border Canada?

A) Atlantic, Arctic and Bering.

B) Atlantic, Arctic and Pacific.

C) Pacific, Indian and Atlantic.

D) Hudson, Pacific and Atlantic.

441- What was the "Underground Railroad"?

A) An anti-slavery network that helped thousands of slaves escape the United States and settle in Canada

B) A railroad through the Rockies that was mainly through mountain tunnels

C) A network fur traders used to transport beaver pelts to the United States

D) The first underground subway tunnel in Toronto

442- What was the significance of June 6, 1944 invasion of Normandy?

A) It led to the establishment of the Juno Awards.

B) It liberated North Africa from Nazi occupation.

C) Canadians made a significant contribution to the defeat of Nazism and Fascism in Europe during the Second World War.

D) It resulted in the forcible relocation of Canadians of Japanese origin.

443- What was the Women's Suffrage Movement?

A) The effort by women to achieve the right to vote.

B) The effort by women to participate in military service.

C) An unsuccessful movement to get husbands to do housework.

D) The effort by women to be in Parliament.

www.toptenaward.org

444- What will you promise when you take the Oath of Citizenship?

A) Pledge allegiance to the King, observe the laws of Canada and fulfil the duties of a Canadian.

B) Pledge to be faithful to the King.

C) Promise to observe the laws of Canada.

D) Fulfil duties as a Canadian citizen.

445- What year did Newfoundland and Labrador join Canada?

A) 1867

B) 1955

C) 1949

D) 1880

446- What year was Confederation?

A) 1867.

B) 1871.

C) 1898.

D) 1864.

447- When asked, who must you tell how you voted in a federal election?

A) Your employer.

B) No one.

C) A police officer.

D) An Elections Canada official.

448- When did the British North America Act come into effect?

A) 1871.

B) 1898.

C) 1867.

D) 1905.

449- When did the Canadian Charter of Rights and Freedoms become part of the Canadian Constitution?

A) 1867.

B) 1905.

C) 1982.

D) 1878.

450- When is Canada Day and what does it celebrate?

A) June 15 of each year to celebrate the anniversary of Confederation.

B) August 8th of each year to celebrate the joining of British Columbia to Confederation.

C) We celebrate the anniversary of Confederation July 1st of each year.

D) May 21st of each year to remember Queen Victoria.

451- When is Remembrance Day celebrated?

A) July 1st

B) October 1st.

C) November 11th.

D) December 25th

452- When must federal elections be held?

A) About every 4 years.

B) On the third Monday in October every four years following the most recent general election.

C) Whenever the Prime Minister calls the election.

D) When the MPs want a new Prime Minister.

453- When you vote on election day, what do you do?

A) Go to the voting station, tell them who you are and mark your X. Give the ballot back to the attendant.

B) Go to the voting station, remove 1 ballot and after marking your X deposit it in the ballot box.

C) Go to the voting station, take your voter's card with proof if identity, highlight your choice on the ballot and deposit it in the box.

D) Go to the voting station with your voter's card and ID, mark an X next to your chosen candidate, fold the ballot and present it to the poll officials who will tear off the ballot number and give you the ballot to deposit in the box

454- Where are the Great Lakes?

A) Between Ontario and the United States

B) Manitoba.

C) Northern Quebec.

D) Atlantic Canada.

455- Where are the Parliament Buildings located?

A) Ottawa.

B) Quebec City.

C) Hull.

D) Toronto.

456- Where do most French-speaking Canadians live?

A) Ontario.

B) Nova Scotia.

C) Quebec.

D) Prince Edward Island.

457- Where does Canada rank in the world's largest countries?

A) First

B) Second

C) Third

D) Fourth

458- Which Act granted, for the first time in Canada, legislative assemblies elected by the people?

A) The Constitutional Act of 1867.

B) The Constitutional Act of 1791.

C) The Constitutional Act of 1982.

D) The Constitutional Act of 2010.

459- Which animal is an official symbol of Canada?

A) The moose.

B) The hawk.

C) The beaver.

D) The deer.

460- Which country borders Canada on the south?

A) United States of America.

B) Central America.

C) Mexico.

D) Washington.

461- Which federal political party is in power?

A) Green Party.

B) New Democratic Party.

C) Liberal Party.

D) Conservative Party.

462- Which of the following is NOT a feature of Canada's system of government?

A) A federal state.

B) Parliamentary democracy.

C) Constitutional Monarchy.

D) Dictatorship.

463 Which of the following sentences best describes the War of 1812?

A) Napoleon's fleet was defeated by the Royal Navy in the war.

B) The USA became independent from the British Empire after the war.

C) The USA invaded Canada and was defeated, which ensured that Canada would remain independent of the United States.

D) Canada joined the United States after the war.

464- Which of the following statements about residential schools is NOT true?

A) The federal government placed many Aboriginal children in residential schools to educate and assimilate them into mainstream Canadian culture.

B) The schools were poorly funded and inflicted hardship on the students.

C) The schools were welcomed by the Aboriginal people.

D) Aboriginal language and cultural practices were mostly prohibited.

465- Which party becomes the Official Opposition?

A) The party with the second most MPs.

B) The party receiving the least votes.

C) Any independent candidate.

D) The party the Prime Minister selects.

466- Which party is the Official Opposition at the federal level?

A) The New Democratic Party.

B) The Liberal Party.

C) The Independent Party.

D) The Conservative Party.

467- Which port is the largest and busiest in Canada?

A) The Port of Halifax

B) The Port of Montreal

C) The Port of Vancouver

D) The Port of Victoria

468- Which province has its own time zone?

A) British Columbia

B) Newfoundland and Labrador

C) Nunavut

D) Nova Scotia

469- Which province in Canada is the smallest in land size?

A) Nova Scotia.

B) Prince Edward Island.

C) Yukon Territory.

D) Newfoundland and Labrador.

470- Which province is the main producer of pulp and paper and hydro-electricity?

A) Quebec

B) Ontario

C) British Columbia

D) Manitoba

471- Which province is the only officially bilingual province?

A) New Brunswick.

B) Quebec.

C) Ontario.

D) Prince Edward Island.

472- Which province was split into two at Confederation?

A) Lower Canada

B) Newfoundland

C) Upper Canada

D) The Province of Canada

473- Which province was the first to grant voting rights to women?

A) Quebec

B) Ontario

C) Nova Scotia

D) Manitoba

474- Which provincial flag features the fleur-de-lys?

A) Quebec

B) New Brunswick

C) Manitoba

D) Ontario

475- Which region covers more than one-third of Canada?

A) Central Canada.

B) Prairies.

C) Atlantic Canada.

D) Northern Territories.

476- Which region is known as the industrial and manufacturing heartland of Canada?

A) Atlantic provinces.

B) Prairie provinces.

C) Central Canada.

D) West Coast.

477- Which region of Canada is known for both its fertile agricultural land and valuable energy resources?

A) British Columbia.

B) Prairie provinces.

C) Ontario.

D) Manitoba.

478- Which three countries are signatories to NAFTA?

A) Canada, the United Kingdom and the United States.

B) Canada, the United States and Japan.

C) Canada, Mexico and the United States.

D) Canada, Denmark and Andorra.

479- Which was the last province to join Canada?

A) Newfoundland.

B) Alberta.

C) Saskatchewan.

D) British Columbia.

480- Who are the Aboriginal peoples of Canada?

A) The first European settlers to arrive in Canada

B) The descendents of the first Australian immigrants to Canada

C) The first people to live in Canada

D) The first settlers of Newfoundland

481- Who are the Acadians?

A) Aboriginal people of the arctic.

B) French-speaking Catholics living in Ontario.

C) The descendants of French colonists who began settling in what are now the Maritime provinces in 1604.

D) English speaking refugees who settled in Louisiana.

482- Who are the founding peoples of Canada?

A) Métis, French and British.

B) Aboriginal, Métis and British.

C) Inuit, Aboriginal and British.

D) Aboriginal, French and British.

483- Who are the Métis?

A) The distinct aboriginal people of Atlantic Canada.

B) A people of mixed Inuit/First Nations ancestry most of whom live on the Prairies.

C) First Nations people speaking the Michif dialect.

D) A distinct people of mixed Aboriginal and European ancestry.

484- Who are the Quebecers?

A) European settlers in the 1600s.

B) Descendants of the French colonists.

C) Descendants of the Anglophones.

D) People of Quebec.

485- Who do Canadians vote for in a federal election?

A) The best speaker running in the election.

B) A candidate they want to represent them in Parliament.

C) Someone to become the Premier.

D) All of the candidates in their electoral district.

486- Who do Members of Parliament represent?

A) All of the Canadians living in the north.

B) Only Canadians living in Central Canada.

C) Everyone who lives in his or her electoral district.

D) Canadians living in the province in which he/she was elected.

487- Who had played an important part in building the Canadian Pacific Railway (CPR)?

A) American railroad engineers.

B) Acadian railroad workers.

C) Chinese railroad workers.

D) African American slaves.

488- Who has the right to run as a candidate in federal elections?

A) Anyone.

B) A Canadian citizen who is 16 years old.

C) Any man who is at least 18 years old.

D) Any Canadian citizen who is at least 18 years old.

www.toptenaward.org

489- Who has the right to vote in federal elections?

A) A Canadian citizen, 18 years or older, and on voters' list.

B) A Canadian citizen, 18 years or older and must work for the federal government.

C) A landed immigrant, 18 years old and a memberof the Canadian Forces.

D) A Canadian citizen, over 25 years and a member of the Canadian Forces.

490- Who have major responsibilities on First Nations reserves?

A) Band chiefs and councillors.

B) Municipal governments.

C) Provincial and territorial governments.

D) Federal government.

491- Who is Canada's Head of State?

A) Governor General of Canada.

B) His Majesty King Charles III.

C) Prime Minister.

D) Lieutenant Governor.

492- Who is considered the father of Manitoba?

A) John A. Macdonald

B) Sam Steele

C) Alfred Boyd

D) Louis Riel

493- Who is General Sir Arthur Currie?

A) A military leader of the Métis in the 19th century.

B) A great frontier hero.

C) An explorer of western Canada.

D) Canada's greatest soldier in the First World War.

494- Who is the Head of Government?

A) The President

B) The King

C) The Governor General

D) The Prime Minister

495- Who is the King's representative in Canada?

A) Prime Minister of Canada.

B) Premier.

C) Lieutenant-Governor.

D) Governor General of Canada.

496- Who is the leader of the Federal Official Opposition Party?

A) Thomas Mulcair

B) Andrew Scheer

C) Pierre Poilievre

D) Elizabeth May

497- Who led an armed uprising and seized Fort Garry?

A) John A. Macdonald

B) Louis Riel

C) Sam Steele

D) George-Étienne Cartier

498- Who led Quebec into Confederation?

A) Sir Louis-Hippolyte La Fontaine

B) Sir George-Étienne Cartier

C) Sir Wilfrid Laurier

D) Sir John A. Macdonald

499- Who was Sir Louis-Hippolyte La Fontaine?

A) A champion of democracy and Aboriginal rights.

B) A champion of democracy and French language rights and the first leader of a responsible government in the Canadas.

C) The first Head of State.

D) The first French speaking Prime Minister.

500- Who was Sir Sam Steele?

A) A great frontier hero, Mounted Policeman and soldier.

B) A military leader of the Métis in the 19th century.

C) The first Prime Minister of Canada.

D) The Father of Manitoba.

501- Who was the first leader of a responsible government in the Canadas in 1849?

A) Sir John A. Macdonald.

B) Robert Baldwin.

C) Louis Riel.

D) Sir Louis-Hippolyte La Fontaine.

502- Who was the first Prime Minister of Canada?

A) Louis Riel.

B) Sir John A. Macdonald.

C) Lester B. Pearson.

D) Abraham Lincoln.

503- Who were the United Empire Loyalists?

A) Settlers who came to Canada from the United States during the American Revolution.

B) Aboriginal peoples.

C) Métis

D) Inuit.

504- Who were the Voyagers?

A) Montreal-based traders who travelled by canoe

B) Immigrants to Canada in the 18th Century

C) Explorers searching for the North-West Passage

D) Geographers who first charted the coastline of British Columbia

505- Why is the battle of Vimy Ridge important?

A) It was a key position of the German line in Northern Spain.

B) Canadian Corps secured its reputation for valour and bravery.

C) It was the "hinge" of the German line as it protected the newly constructed Hindenburg line.

D) Once Canadians fought at Vimy they knew they would be heading home.

506- Why is trade with other countries important to Canada?

A) It enhances our standard of living.

B) It makes it easier for us to travel to foreign countries.

C) It enhances our economy and raises our standard of living.

D) It brings in cheaper goods.

507- What is the name of the Lieutenant-Governor of Quebec?

A) Honourable Pierre Duchesne

B) Honourable Jean-Louis Roux

C) Honourable Martial Asselin

D) Honourable J. Michel Doyon

508- What is the capital city of Alberta?

A) Medicine Hat.

B) Red Deer.

C) Calgary.

D) Edmonton.

509- What is the name of the leader of the Opposition in Alberta?

A) Rachel Notley.

B) Brian Jean.

C) Heather Forsyth.

D) Jim Prentice.

510- What is the name of the Lieutenant-Governor of Alberta?

A) Donald S. Ethell.

B) Salma Lakhani.

C) Adrienne Clarkson.

D) Lois Mitchell.

511- What is the name of the Premier of Alberta?

A) Premier Rachel Notley.

B) Premier Jason Kenney.

C) Premier Jim Prentice.

D) Premier Stephen Harper

512- Which political party is in power in Alberta?

A) New Democratic Party.

B) Liberal Party.

C) Green Party.

D) United Conservative Party

513- Which three natural resources are important to Alberta's economy today?

A) Oil, agriculture, and forestry.

B) Oil, tourism, and fishing.

C) Oil, coal, and hydroelectricity.

D) Oil, coal, and forestry.

www.toptenaward.org

514- Name the federal electoral districts in Richmond, British Columbia.

A) Richmond has two federal electoral districts: Richmond North and Richmond South

B) Richmond has two federal electoral districts: Richmond East and Richmond West

C) Richmond has two federal electoral districts: Richmond and Richmond South.

D) Richmond has two federal electoral districts: Richmond Centre and Steveston-Richmond East

515- Name the members of Parliament for Richmond, British Columbia and the parties they belong to (Richmond Centre, Steveston-Richmond East respectively).

A) Alice Wong (Conservative), Kenny Chiu (Conservative)

B) Joe Peschisolido (Liberal), Kerry-Lynne Findlay (Conservative)

C) Wilson Miao (Liberal), Parm Bains (Liberal)

D) Greg Halsey-Brandt (Liberal), Geoff Plant (Liberal)

516- Name the Members of the Legislative Assembly for Richmond, British Columbia and the parties they belong to (Richmond North Centre, Richmond South Centre, Richmond-Steveston, and Richmond-Queensborough respectively).

A) Rob Howard (Richmond North Centre), Linda Reid (Richmond South Centre), John Cummins (Richmond-Steveston), and Malcolm Brodie (Richmond-Queensborough)

B) Teresa Wat (Richmond North Centre), Linda Reid (Richmond South Centre), John Yap (Richmond-Steveston), and Jas Johal (Richmond-Queensborough)

C) Olga Ilich (Richmond North Centre), Rob Howard (Richmond South Centre), Jas Johal (Richmond-Steveston), and John Yap (Richmond-Queensborough)

D) Teresa Wat (Richmond North Centre), Henry Yao (Richmond South Centre), Kelly Greene(Richmond-Steveston), Aman Singh (Richmond-Queensborough).

517- Name three city councilors for Richmond, British Columbia.

- A) Malcolm Brodie, Derek Dang and Ernie Novakowski

- B) Lyn Greenhill, Kiichi Kumagai and Lily von Hendron

- C) Harold Steves, Chak Au and Carol Day

- D) Ken Johnston, Bill McNulty and Lee Bailey

518- What is the capital city of British Columbia?

- A) Vancouver.

- B) Prince George.

- C) Victoria.

- D) New Westminster.

519- What is the name of the leader of the Opposition in British Columbia?

- A) Adam Olsen

- B) Kevin Falcon

- C) John Horgan

- D) Andrew Wilkinson

520- What is the name of the Lieutenant-Governor of British Columbia?

A) David Lam

B) Janet Austin

C) Adrienne Clarkson

D) Judith Guichon

521- What is the name of the Mayor of Richmond, British Columbia?

A) Mayor Richard Lee

B) Mayor Bill McNulty

C) Mayor Linda McPhail

D) Mayor Malcolm Brodie

522- What is the name of the Premier of British Columbia?

A) Premier Adrian Dix

B) Premier Gordon Campbell

C) Premier John Horgan

D) Premier Christy Clark

523- Which political party is in power in British Columbia?

A) New Democratic Party

B) Liberal Party

C) Social Credit Party

D) Green Party

524- Which three natural resources are important to British Columbia's economy today?

A) Forests, water and grain crops.

B) Forests, fish and water.

C) Fish, oil and water.

D) Coal, water and shipbuilding.

525- Why is British Columbia known as Canada's Pacific Gateway?

A) Most new imigrants arrive at Vancouver International Airport.

B) British Columbia is the closest province to the Far East.

C) Billions of dollars in trade goods are handled through the Port of Vancouver.

D) British Columbia borders the Pacific Ocean.

526- What is the capital city of Manitoba?

A) Winnipeg

B) Grand Rapids

C) Portage la Prairie

D) Brandon

527- What is the name of the leader of the Opposition in Manitoba?

A) Rana Bokhari

B) James Beddome

C) Wab Kinew

D) Brian Pallister

528- What is the name of the Lieutenant-Governor of Manitoba?

A) Honourable John Harvard

B) Honourable Peter Liba

C) Honourable Philip Lee

D) Honourable Janice Filmon

529- What is the name of the Premier of Manitoba?

A) Premier Heather Stefanson

B) Premier Greg Selinger

C) Premier Brian Pallister

D) Premier Sterling Lyon

530- What three industries are important to Manitoba's economy today?

A) Farming, mining and fishing

B) Agriculture, mining and hydro-electric power generation

C) Fishing, tourism and mining

D) Forestry, fishing and energy

531- Which political party is in power in Manitoba?

A) Manitoba Party

B) Liberals

C) Progressive Conservative

D) New Democrats

532- What is the capital city of
New Brunswick?

A) Victoria

B) Winnipeg

C) Fredericton

D) Montreal

533- What is the name of the leader of the
Opposition in New Brunswick?

A) Victor Boudreau

B) Denis Landry

C) Roger Melanson

D) David Alward

534- What is the name of the Lieutenant-Governor of New Brunswick?

A) Honourable Brenda Murphy

B) Honourable Gilbert Finn

C) Honourable Marilyn Trenholme Counsell

D) Honourable Graydon Nicholas

535- What is the name of the Premier of New Brunswick?

A) Premier Bernard Lord

B) Premier Blaine Higgs

C) Premier David Alward

D) Premier Brian Gallant

536- What three industries are important to New Brunswick's economy today?

A) Forestry, hydro-electric power generation, oil

B) Fisheries, oil, tourism

C) Atlantic trade, fishing and oil

D) Forestry, agriculture and mining

537- Which political party is in power in New Brunswick?

A) Liberals

B) New Brunswick Party

C) New Democrats

D) Progressive Conservative

538- What is the capital city of Newfoundland and Labrador?

A) Charlottetown

B) Chimney Tickle

C) St. John's

D) St. Pierre et Miquelon

539- What is the name of the leader of the Opposition in Newfoundland and Labrador?

A) David Brazil

B) Ches Crosbie

C) Paul Davis

D) Dwight Ball

540- What is the name of the Lieutenant-Governor of Newfoundland and Labrador?

A) Honourable Frank F. Fagan

B) Honourable Edward Roberts

C) Honourable John Crosbie

D) Honourable Judy May Foote

541- What is the name of the Premier of New-foundland and Labrador?

A) Premier Andrew Furey

B) Premier Dwight Ball

C) Premier Kathy Dunderdale

D) Premier Tom Marshall

542- What three industries are important to Newfoundland and Labrador's economy today?

A) Fisheries, oil and gas extraction

B) Fisheries, tourism, forestry

C) Shipbuilding, fisheries and mining

D) Tourism, mining and forestry

543- Which political party is in power in Newfoundland and Labrador?

A) NFL Party

B) New Democrats

C) Liberal Party

D) Progressive Conservative

544- What is the capital City of Nova Scotia?

A) Shearwater

B) Halifax

C) Dartmouth

D) Devon

545- What is the name of the leader of the Opposition in Nova Scotia?

A) Darrell Dexter

B) John MacDonell

C) Iain Rankin

D) Jamie Baillie

546- What is the name of the Lieutenant-Governor of Nova Scotia?

A) Honourable John James Grant

B) Honourable Myra Freeman

C) Honourable Mayann Francis

D) Honourable Arthur J. LeBlanc

547- What is the name of the Premier of Nova Scotia?

A) Premier Darrel Dexter

B) Premier Stephen McNeil

C) Premier Tim Houston

D) Premier Rodney MacDonald

548- What three industries are important to Nova Scotia's economy today?

A) Fisheries, shipbuilding and forestry

B) Forestry, mining and tourism

C) Coal mining, forestry and agriculture

D) Tourism, movies and shipbuilding

549- Which political party is in power in Nova Scotia?

A) New Democrats

B) Progressive Conservative

C) Liberal

D) Nova Scotia Party

550- What is the capital City of the Northwest Territories?

A) Fort Simpson

B) Hay River

C) Fort Providence

D) Yellowknife

551- What is the name of the Commissioner of the Northwest Territories?

A) Honourable Margaret Thom

B) Honourable Tony Whitford

C) Honourable Daniel L. Norris

D) Honourable Glenna Hansen

552- What is the name of the leader of the Opposition in the Northwest Territories?

A) None

B) George Braden

C) Don Morin

D) Nellie Cournoyea

553- What is the name of the Premier of the Northwest Territories?

A) Premier Bob McLeod

B) Premier Caroline Cochrane

C) Premier Joe Handley

D) Premier Jim Antoine

554- Which political party is in power in the Northwest Territories?

A) Yukon Party

B) Liberals

C) Governed by consensus

D) New Democrats

555- What is the capital City of the Nunavut?

A) Sinaa

B) Iqaluit

C) Nipisa

D) Mivvik

556- What is the name of the Commissioner of Nunavut?

A) Honourable Peter Irniq

B) Honourable Ann Meekitjuk Hanson

C) Honourable Eva Aariak

D) Honourable Nellie Taptaqut Kusugak

557- What is the name of the leader of the Opposition in Nunavut?

A) Don Morin

B) Joe Handley

C) None

D) Eva Aariak

558- What is the name of the Premier of Nunavut?

A) Premier Paul Okalik

B) Premier Floyd Roalnd

C) Premier Joe Savikataaq

D) Premier P.J. Akeeagok

559- Which political party is in power in Nunavut?

A) Progressive Conservative

B) Liberal

C) Nunavut Party

D) Governed by consensus

560- What is the capital city of Ontario?

A) Kingston

B) Ottawa

C) Toronto

D) London

561- What is the name of the leader of the Opposition in Ontario?

A) Andrea Horwath

B) Tim Hudak

C) Peter Tabuns

D) Dalton McGuinty

562- What is the name of the Lieutenant-Governor of Ontario?

A) James Bartleman

B) Elizabeth Dowdeswell

C) David C. Onley

D) Belinda Stronach

563- What is the name of the Premier of Ontario?

A) Premier Doug Ford

B) Premier Jack Layton

C) Premier Kathleen Wynne

D) Premier Mike Harris

564- What three industries are important to Ontario's economy today?

A) Mining, fishing, automobile manufacturing

B) Mining, tourism, automobile manufacturing

C) Farming, tourism, fishing

D) Automobile manufacturing, tourism, fishing

565- Which political party is in power in Ontario?

A) Green Party

B) Liberal Party

C) Progressive Conservative Party

D) New Democratic Party

566- Which three are Members of Ontario's Legislative Assembly?

A) Brian Kilrea, Marlene Catterall, Tom Green

B) Howard Hampton, Maurice Richard, Daniel Poliquin

C) Daniel Lanois, Rosario Marchese, Diane Dufresne

D) Paul Calandra, Todd Smith, Lisa Gretzky

212 • MAHNAZ WAEZI

567- What is the capital City of the Prince Edward Island?

A) Cornwall

B) Stratford

C) Charlottetown

D) Georgetown

568- What is the name of the leader of the Opposition in Prince Edward Island?

A) Olive Crane

B) Jamie Fox

C) Steven Meyers

D) Peter Bevan-Baker

569- What is the name of the Lieutenant-Governor of Prince Edward Island?

A) Honourable Antoinette Perry

B) Honourable H. Frank Lewis

C) Honourable Barbara Oliver Hagerman

D) Honourable Léonce Barnard

570- What is the name of the Premier of Prince Edward Island?

A) Premier Wade MacLauchlan

B) Premier Dennis King

C) Premier Pat Binns

D) Premier Joe Ghiz

571-Which political party is in power in Prince Edward Island?

A) Progressive Conservative

B) New Democrats

C) Liberals

D) Union Nationale

572-What is the capital City of the Quebec?

A) Beauport

B) Quebec City

C) Montreal

D) Chicoutimi

573- What is the name of the leader of the Opposition in Quebec?

A) Dominique Anglade

B) Pierre Arcand

C) Jean-Marc Fournie

D) Philippe Couillard

574- What is the name of the Premier of Quebec ?

A) Premier Lucien Bouchard

B) Premier Pauline Marois

C) Premier Francois Legault

D) Premier Philippe Couillard

575- What three industries are important to Quebec's economy today?

A) Tourism, mining and forestry

B) Pulp and paper, forestry and hydro-electric power

C) Films, fishing and mining

D) Forestry, shipping and tourism

576- Which political party is in power in Quebec?

A) Coalition Avenir Québec

B) Parti libéral

C) Parti Quebecois

D) Union Nationale

577- What is the capital city of Saskatche-wan?

A) Regina

B) Avonlea

C) Glenavon

D) Fort Qu'Appelle

578- What three industries are important to Saskatchewan's economy today?

A) Forestry, films and tourism

B) Fishing, mining and agriculture

C) Mining, oil production and forestry

D) Farming, mining and natural gas

579- What is the capital city of Yukon Territory?

A) MacRae

B) Crestview

C) Whitehorse

D) Riverdale

580- What is the name of the Commissioner of Yukon Territory?

A) Honourable Doug Phillips

B) Honourable Angélique Bernard

C) Honourable Jack Cable

D) Honourable Douglas Bell

581- Which of the following are two words that can be used instead of the words king or queen?

A) monarch

B) Sovereign

C) Premier

D) monarch or sovereign

582- What three terms can you use to describe the form of government Canada has?

A) constitutional monarchy

B) parliamentary democracy

C) federal state

D) dictatorship

583- How many years have settlers and immigrants come to this country?

A) 100 years

B) 200 years

C) 300 years

D) 400 years

584- There are (4) fundamental freedoms that Canadians enjoy. Which choice is not correct?

A) freedom of peaceful assembly

B) freedom of association

C) freedom of peaceful assembly

D) freedom to own guns

585- When was the Constitution of Canada changed?

    A) 1870

    B) 1882

    C) 1970

    D) 1982

586- Who has to obey the law?

    A) men

    B) women

    C) children

    D) everyone

587- What is meant by the equality of men and women?

    A) Men provide for women.

    B) They care for each other.

    C) Women provide for men.

    D) Men and women are equal under the law.

588- What does a jury do?

A) helps the police

B) helps the judge

C) helps the lawyer

D) helps the immigrants

589- What are the three kinds of elections?

A) State, county and area

B) State, provincial and local

C) Federal, provincial or territorial, local

D) Federal, state, and local

590- Do you have to join the Canadian army?

A) yes, after the age of 18

B) yes, after the age of 21

C) yes, but only men

D) no

591- What are the advantages of volunteering? (Pick three)

A) You can make money.

B) All of them

C) You can make friends.

D) You can network for jobs.

592- Who are the Métis? (Who are they descended from?)

A) Spanish & French

B) English & Aboriginal

C) English & French and ABoriginal

D) French & Aboriginal

593- Who were the first people to live in Canada?

A) the Aboriginal

B) the Spanish

C) the French

D) the British

594- What did Canada apologize for in 2008?

A) the railroad

B) the Japanese internment

C) the Head Tax

D) residential schools

595- What does the word "Inuit" mean?

A) the people

B) the Night

C) a new day

D) | knew it

Online Canadian Citizenship Practice Test
www.toptenaward.org

1	D	24	A	47	C	70	A	93	D
2	A	25	B	48	B	71	A	94	D
3	C	26	A	49	A	72	A	95	A
4	A	27	A	50	A	73	D	96	C
5	A	28	D	51	D	74	A	97	B
6	B	29	A	52	B	75	A	98	A
7	A	30	A	53	C	76	A	99	B
8	B	31	A	54	C	77	D	100	B
9	A	32	B	55	A	78	A	101	D
10	A	33	C	56	B	79	A	102	A
11	A	34	B	57	A	80	D	103	A
12	A	35	C	58	A	81	B	104	A
13	A	36	B	59	A	82	C	105	A
14	C	37	A	60	A	83	A	106	C
15	A	38	A	61	A	84	D	107	B
16	A	39	D	62	C	85	A	108	A
17	C	40	A	63	A	86	B	109	D
18	D	41	C	64	A	87	C	110	B
19	B	42	D	65	B	88	A	111	D
20	D	43	B	66	C	89	A	112	C
21	A	44	B	67	D	90	B	113	A
22	C	45	A	68	C	91	A	114	A
23	C	46	D	69	A	92	B	115	B

116	C	139	B	162	D	185	B	208	B
117	B	140	A	163	A	186	D	209	B
118	A	141	A	164	B	187	A	210	A
119	A	142	C	165	B	188	C	211	A
120	D	143	A	166	A	189	B	212	D
121	A	144	B	167	B	190	C	213	C
122	C	145	C	168	D	191	A	214	A
123	B	146	A	169	A	192	B	215	C
124	C	147	A	170	C	193	A	216	A
125	A	148	B	171	A	194	C	217	B
126	B	149	C	172	A	195	B	218	D
127	D	150	C	173	B	196	A	219	A
128	A	151	B	174	D	197	D	220	B
129	A	152	A	175	C	198	B	221	A
130	A	153	D	176	B	199	A	222	A
131	C	154	C	177	A	200	A	223	B
132	B	155	A	178	A	201	A	224	B
133	B	156	A	179	D	202	D	225	C
134	D	157	C	180	A	203	D	226	A
135	A	158	A	181	D	204	D	227	C
136	A	159	B	182	A	205	B	228	A
137	C	160	B	183	C	206	A	229	D
138	A	161	B	184	A	207	A	230	B

231	A	254	C	277	D	300	D	323	B
232	B	255	A	278	C	301	D	324	A
233	B	256	B	279	A	302	A	325	D
234	A	257	A	280	C	303	A	326	C
235	B	258	D	281	B	304	C	327	A
236	A	259	D	282	D	305	A	328	C
237	C	260	C	283	C	306	B	329	D
238	D	261	A	284	B	307	C	330	B
239	B	262	A	285	D	308	A	331	D
240	A	263	C	286	A	309	D	332	C
241	A	264	D	287	D	310	C	333	B
242	D	265	B	288	D	311	B	334	D
243	D	266	C	289	C	312	A	335	A
244	A	267	A	290	A	313	A	336	C
245	D	268	D	291	D	314	B	337	B
246	A	269	C	292	B	315	D	338	D
247	B	270	A	293	B	316	A	339	A
248	A	271	C	294	C	317	C	340	A
249	C	272	C	295	B	318	A	341	D
250	D	273	C	296	D	319	C	342	A
251	A	274	A	297	C	320	C	343	C
252	A	275	A	298	B	321	C	344	A
253	A	276	B	299	D	322	A	345	A

346	D	369	A	392	B	415	C	438	D
347	B	370	B	393	B	416	B	439	B
348	D	371	D	394	C	417	D	440	B
349	D	372	B	395	B	418	C	441	A
350	D	373	D	396	D	419	D	442	C
351	B	374	B	397	A	420	B	443	A
352	B	375	C	398	A	421	A	444	A
353	C	376	D	399	D	422	A	445	C
354	A	377	D	400	D	423	A	446	A
355	A	378	C	401	C	424	B	447	B
356	D	379	C	402	B	425	C	448	C
357	B	380	A	403	C	426	C	449	C
358	C	381	A	404	A	427	D	450	C
359	C	382	D	405	C	428	A	451	C
360	C	383	C	406	C	429	D	452	B
361	C	384	B	407	C	430	B	453	D
362	A	385	A	408	D	431	A	454	A
363	D	386	C	409	B	432	B	455	A
364	B	387	B	410	C	433	C	456	C
365	A	388	B	411	C	434	C	457	B
366	D	389	B	412	C	435	B	458	B
367	D	390	B	413	C	436	D	459	C
368	C	391	B	414	C	437	D	460	A

461	C	484	D	507	D	530	B	553	B
462	D	485	B	508	D	531	C	554	C
463	C	486	C	509	A	532	C	555	B
464	C	487	C	510	B	533	C	556	D
465	A	488	D	511	B	534	A	557	C
466	D	489	A	512	D	535	B	558	D
467	C	490	A	513	A	536	D	559	D
468	B	491	B	514	D	537	D	560	C
469	B	492	D	515	C	538	C	561	C
470	A	493	D	516	D	539	A	562	B
471	A	494	D	517	C	540	D	563	A
472	D	495	D	518	C	541	A	564	B
473	D	496	C	519	B	542	A	565	C
474	A	497	B	520	B	543	C	566	D
475	D	498	B	521	D	544	B	567	C
476	C	499	B	522	C	545	C	568	D
477	B	500	A	523	A	546	D	569	A
478	C	501	D	524	B	547	C	570	B
479	A	502	B	525	C	548	C	571	A
480	C	503	A	526	A	549	B	572	B
481	C	504	A	527	C	550	D	573	A
482	D	505	B	528	D	551	A	574	A
483	D	506	C	529	A	552	A	575	B

576	A
577	A
578	D
579	C
580	B
581	D
582	D
583	D
584	D
585	D
586	D
587	D
588	B
589	C
590	D
591	B
592	C
593	A
594	D
595	A

Test Your CanadianCitizenship knowledge here:

www.toptenaward.org

GOOD
LUCK

www.ingramcontent.com/pod-product-compliance
Lightning Source LLC
Chambersburg PA
CBHW071319120626
46546CB00002B/377